Pantagruelian

Photographs and Poems of Torres del Paine

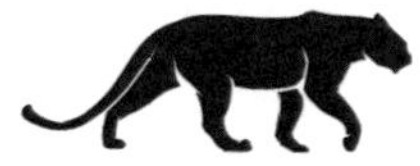

Paul Brooke

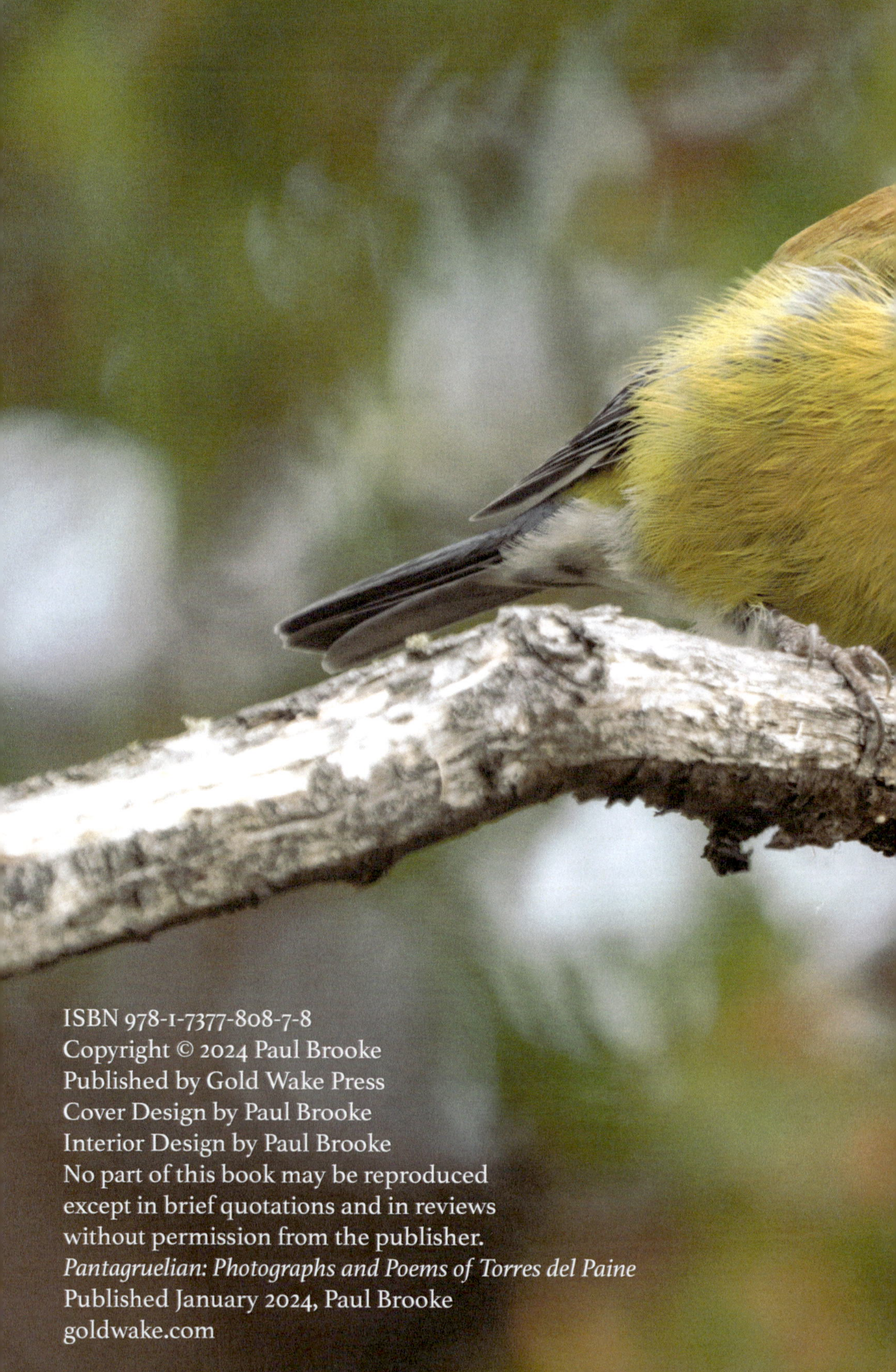

ISBN 978-1-7377-808-7-8

Published by Gold Wake Press
Cover Design by Paul Brooke
Interior Design by Paul Brooke

Pantagruelian: Photographs and Poems of Torres del Paine
Published January 2024, Paul Brooke
goldwake.com

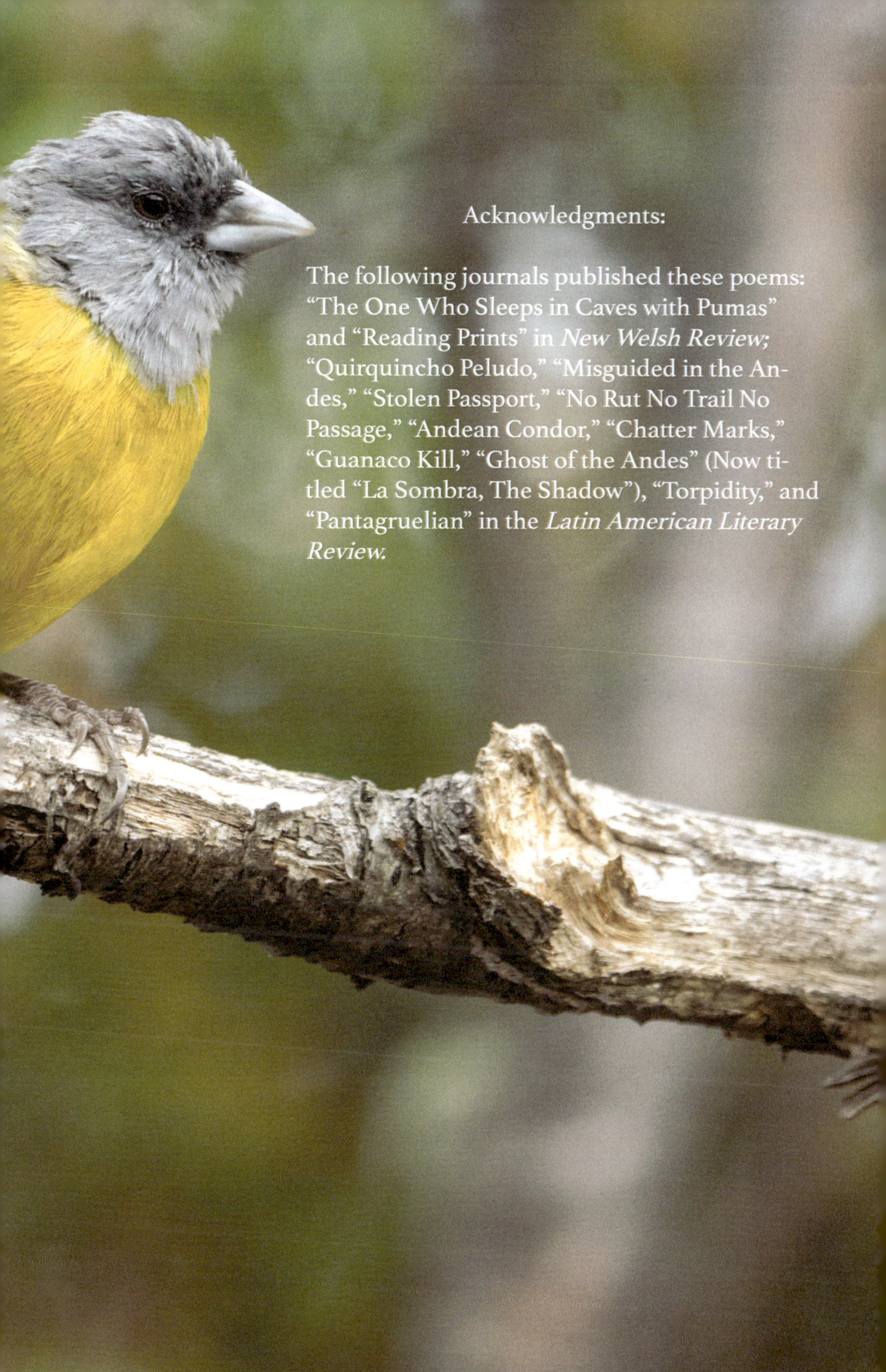
Acknowledgments:

The following journals published these poems: "The One Who Sleeps in Caves with Pumas" and "Reading Prints" in *New Welsh Review;* "Quirquincho Peludo," "Misguided in the Andes," "Stolen Passport," "No Rut No Trail No Passage," "Andean Condor," "Chatter Marks," "Guanaco Kill," "Ghost of the Andes" (Now titled "La Sombra, The Shadow"), "Torpidity," and "Pantagruelian" in the *Latin American Literary Review.*

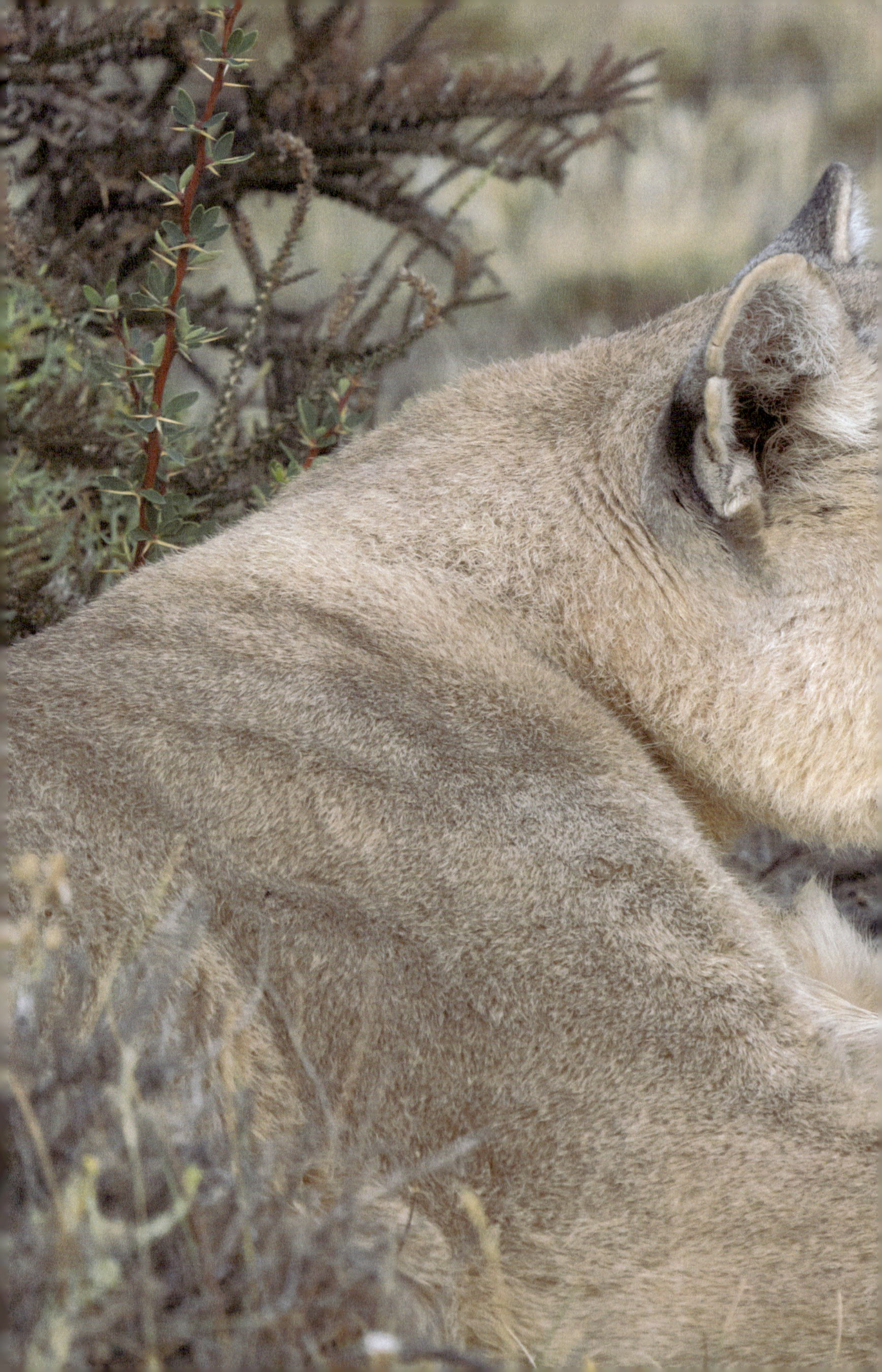

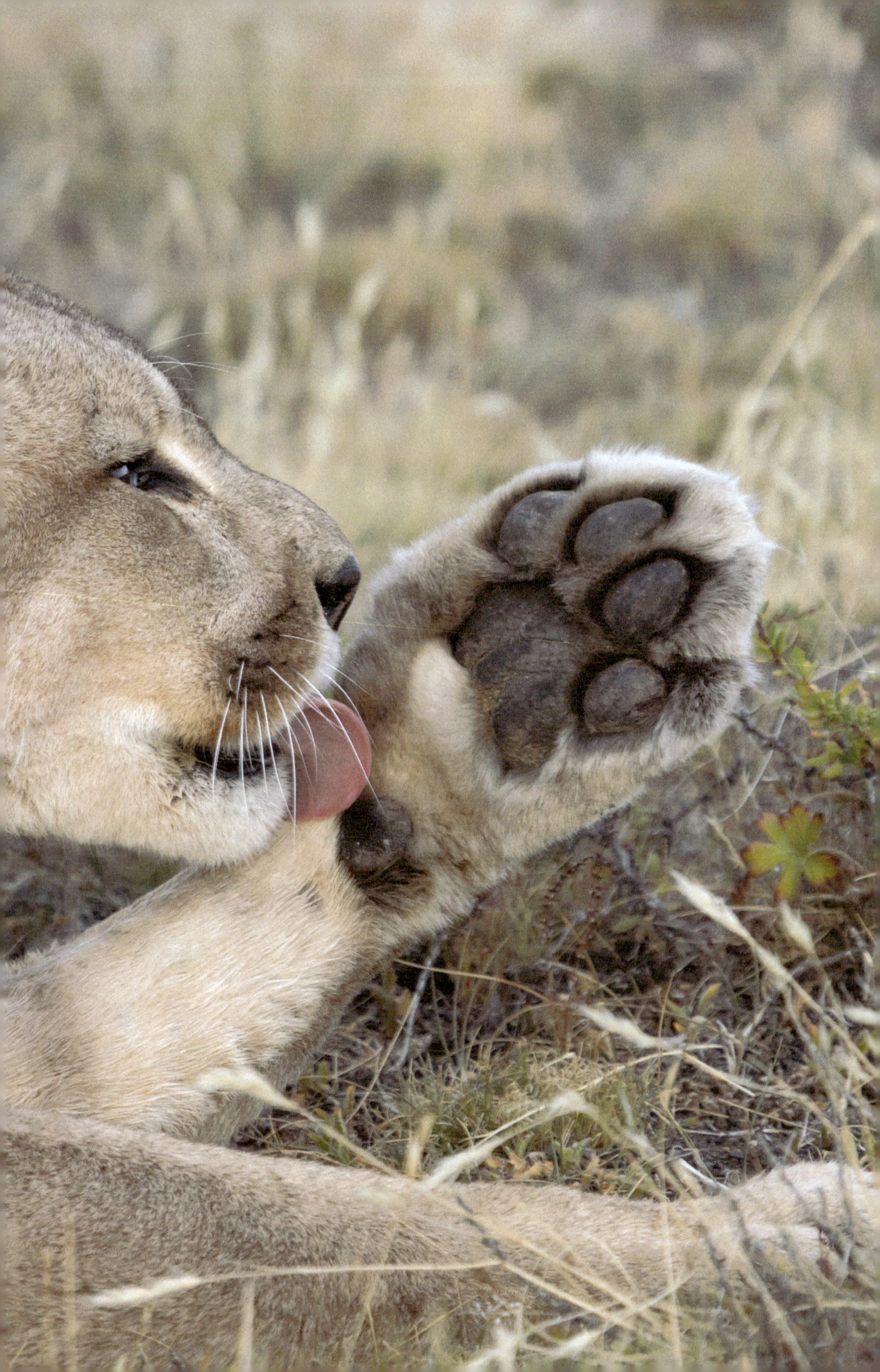

Table of Contents

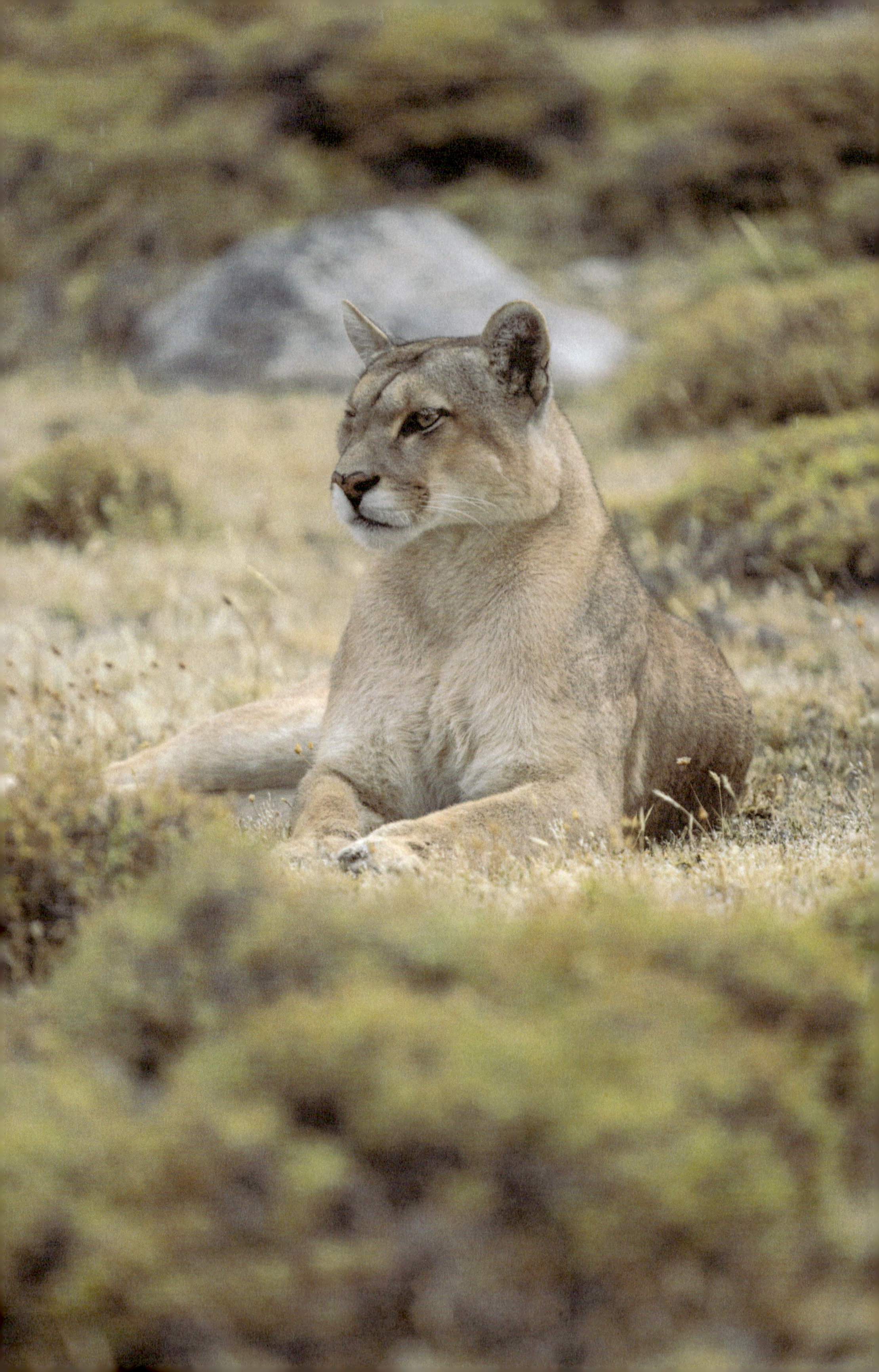

For Javiera Vargas and Junior Mendes

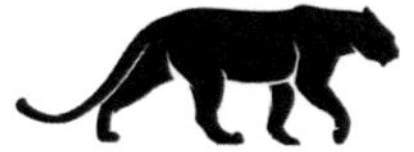

The Flamingos of the Atacama Desert

No, flamingos (she thought) survived worse:
Endured salt flats, hellish heat;
Sucked diatoms in boiling water;
Stirred winter ice with feet.
Yes, stirred winter ice with feet.
And yet brine shrimp turn their feathers pink.
At the click of the latch, she waded
To avoid his cruel words, his reach.

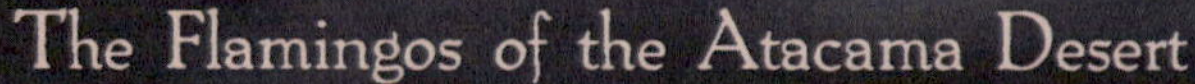

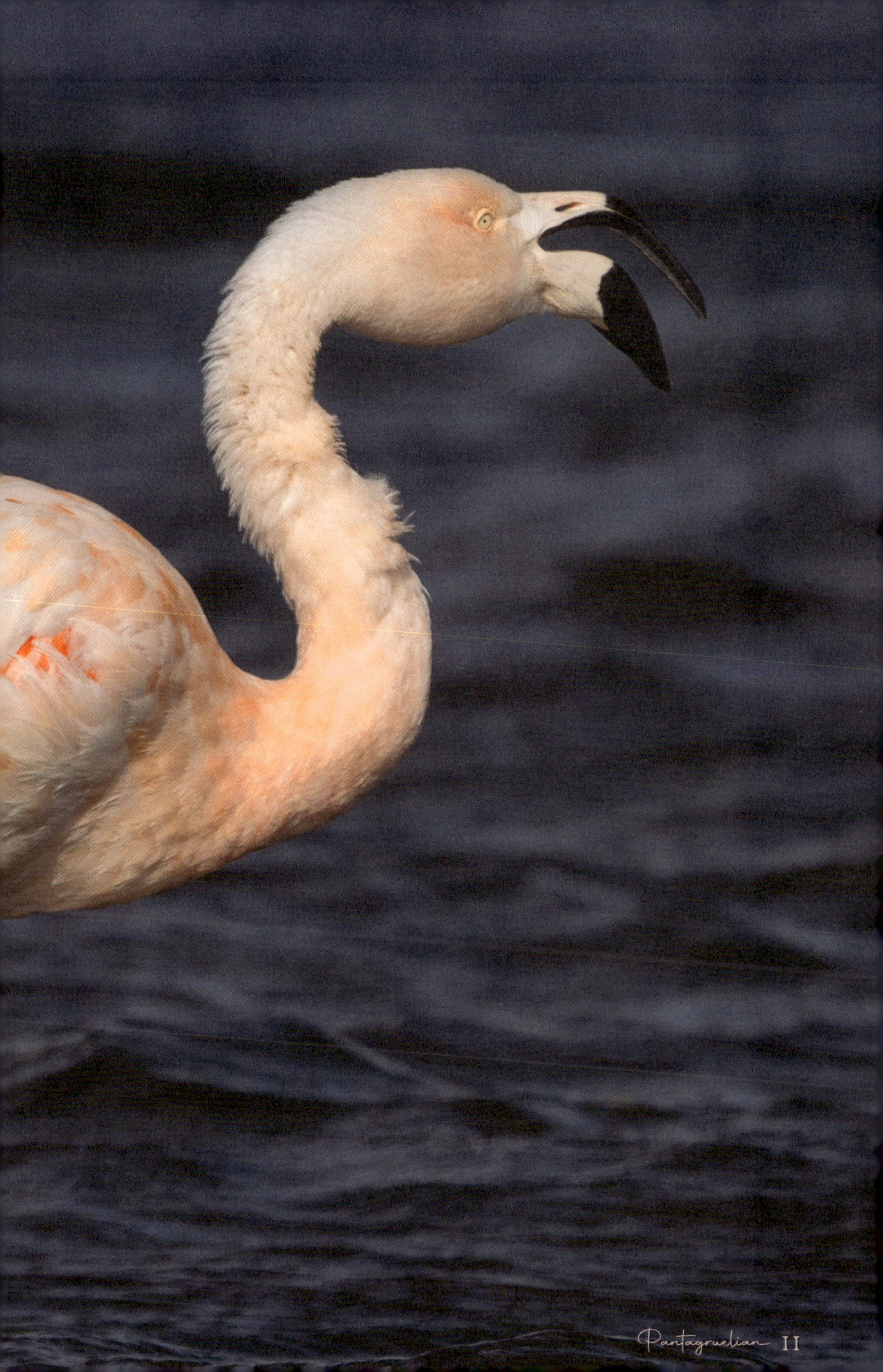
Pantagruelian II

Crested Duck

No, she sought identity of he.
In Rio Ascencio,
Two ducks clung to the side of slick rock,
Immune to the undertow.
Yes, immune to the undertow.
Tourists applauded and praised aloud.
Despite dense anger met on the streets,
She plunged and pushed through the callous crowds.

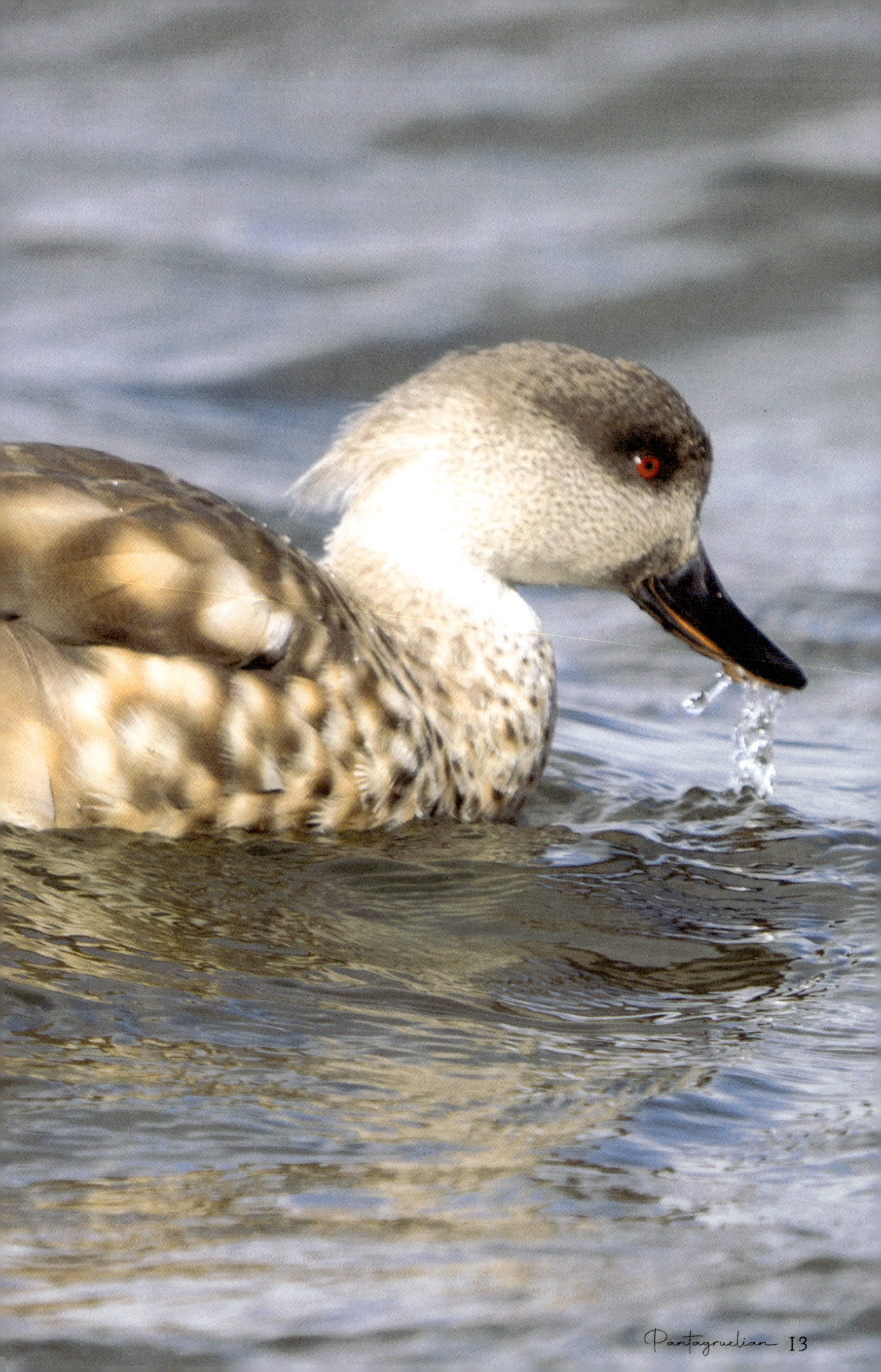
Pantagruelian 13

Quirquincho Peludo

She unhurriedly unwound, sketching
Woodpeckers, rock earthcreepers
And armadillos. A quirquincho
Unrolled from a ball, reassured,
Yes, unrolled from a ball, reassured,
Not fainthearted around multitudes.
With drawing, the girl unfurled further,
Ending her enduring solitude.

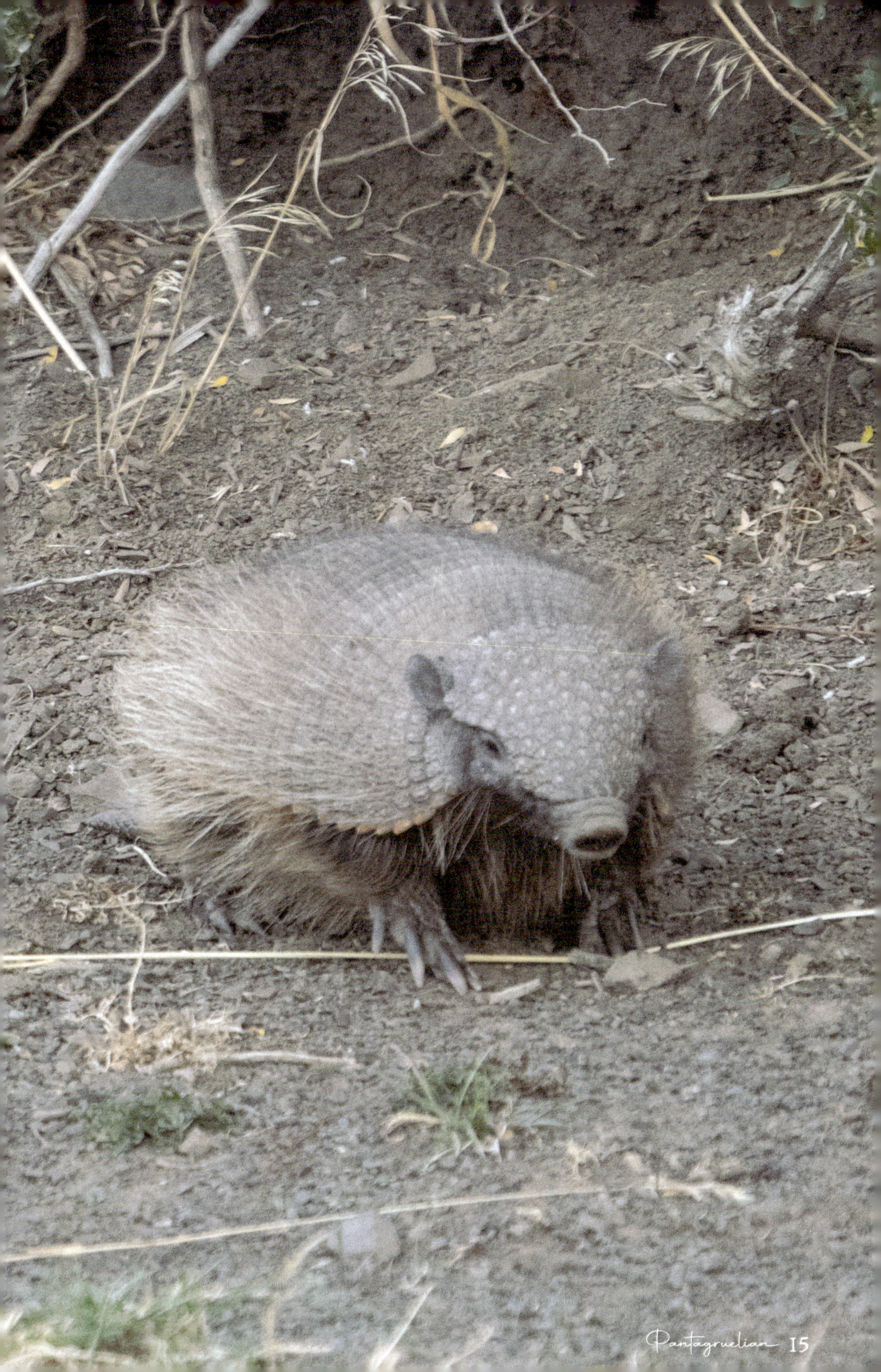
Pantagruelian 15

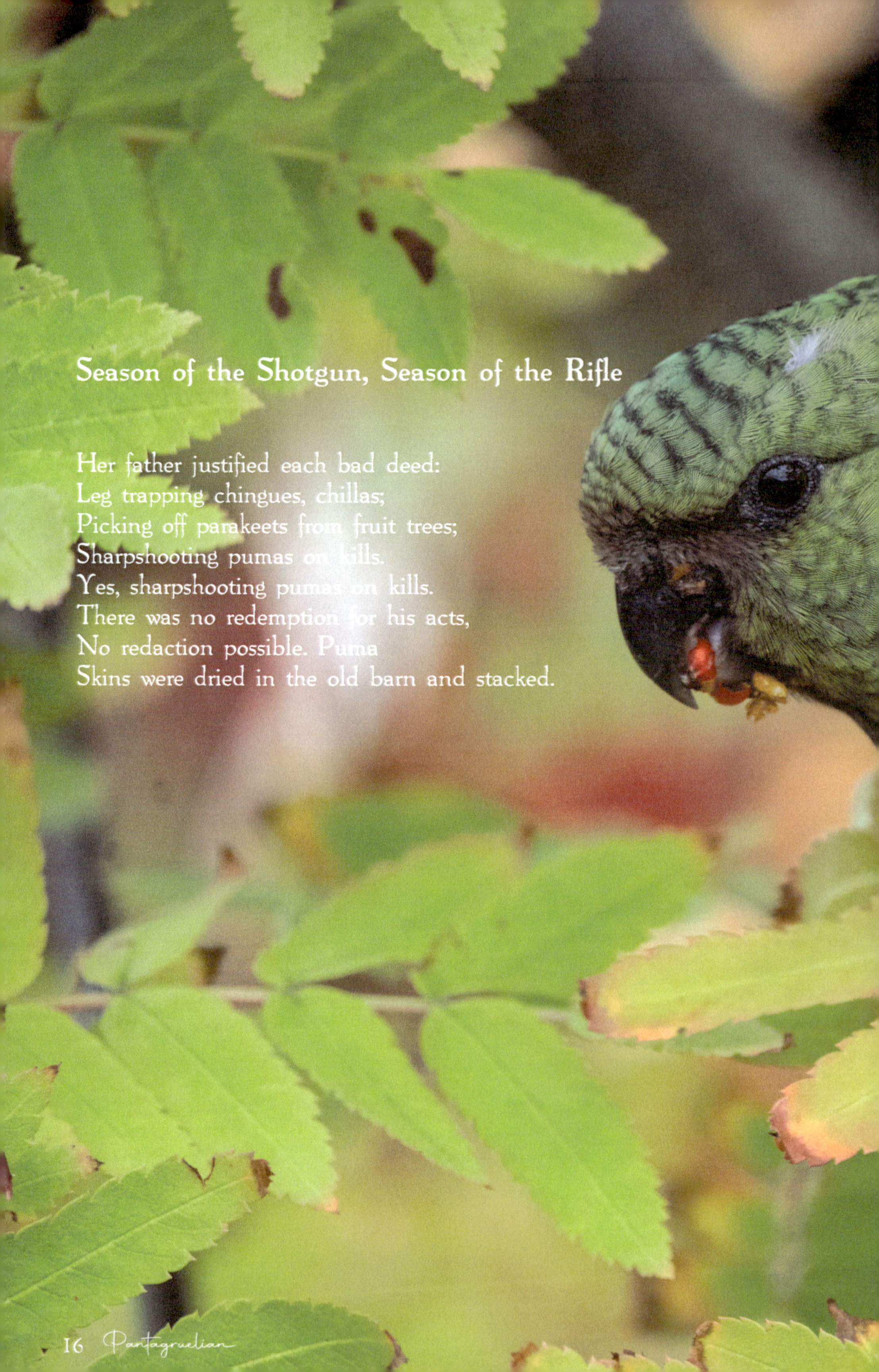

Season of the Shotgun, Season of the Rifle

Her father justified each bad deed:
Leg trapping chingues, chillas;
Picking off parakeets from fruit trees;
Sharpshooting pumas on kills.
Yes, sharpshooting pumas on kills.
There was no redemption for his acts,
No redaction possible. Puma
Skins were dried in the old barn and stacked.

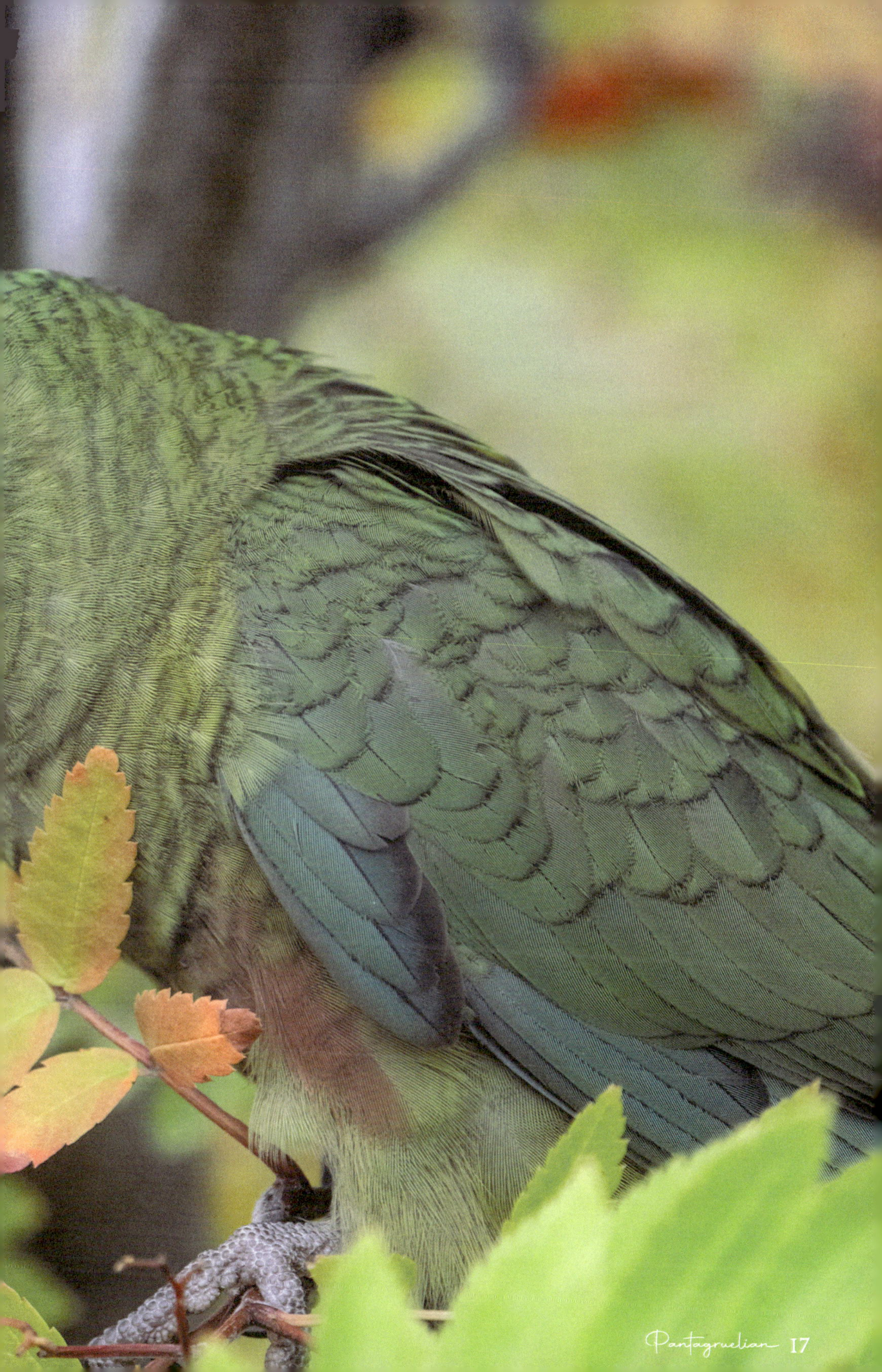
Pantagruelian 17

Misguided in the Andes

Brothers rebuffed. *La mujer llorò.*
No penguins at Isla Foca.
Fogged in mountains at Torres del Paine.
The guide never tracked pumas,
Si, the guide never tracked pumas.
But unlocked rocks and faced ice-shard winds.
She regretted her feeble choice,
Blazed a trail herself through the unkind.

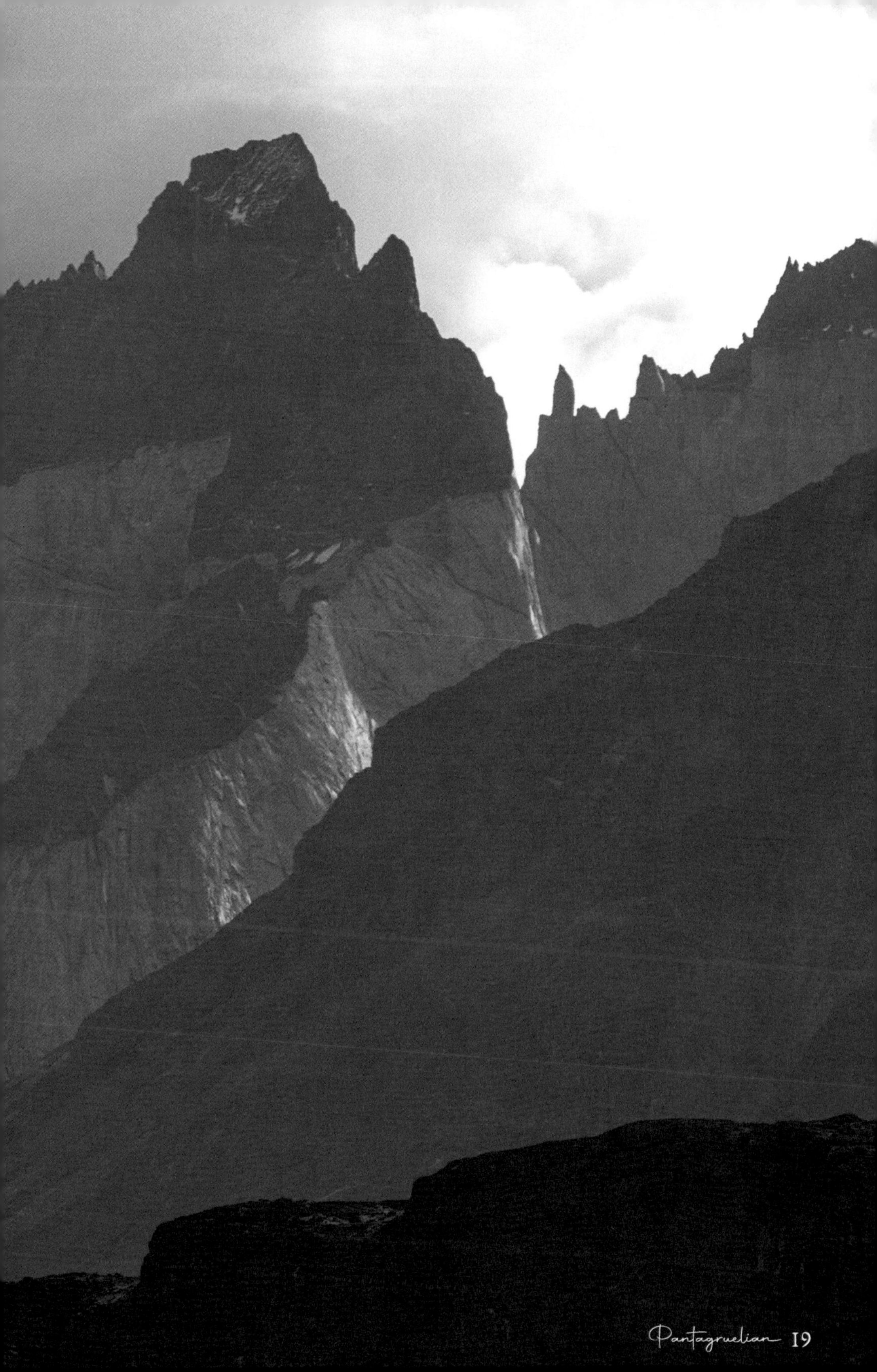
Pantagruelian 19

Unsafe

Safe in her hotel room ransacked.
She scoured grasses for cache
Under Blue Towers' hocked hills.
Winds slanted like a backslash.
Yes, winds slanted like a backslash.
Guanacos grazed in small herds.
Stone broke without prospect, in limbo,
She imagined suicide, unnerved

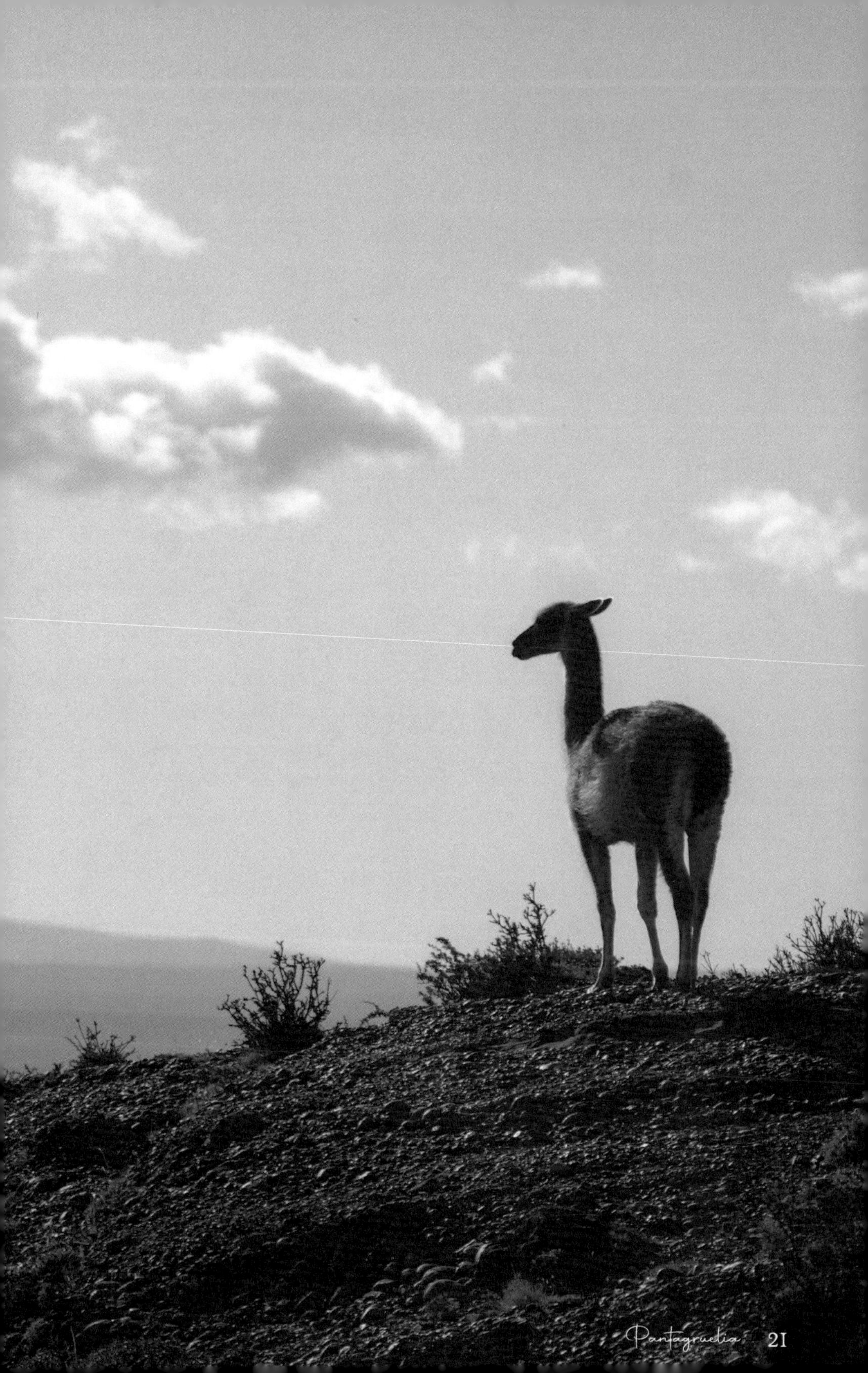
Pantagruelix
21

No Rut No Trail No Passage

"No, mom, I don't want to talk to you."
She wandered among blue stones,
Rag winds and snow. No one to follow.
Zigzagging through ribs and gnawed bones.
Yes, zigzagging through ribs and gnawed bones.
Strip down and freeze? Step off cliff and fall?
"Will my girl cry softly? Sob wildly?
Will she think fondly of me at all?"

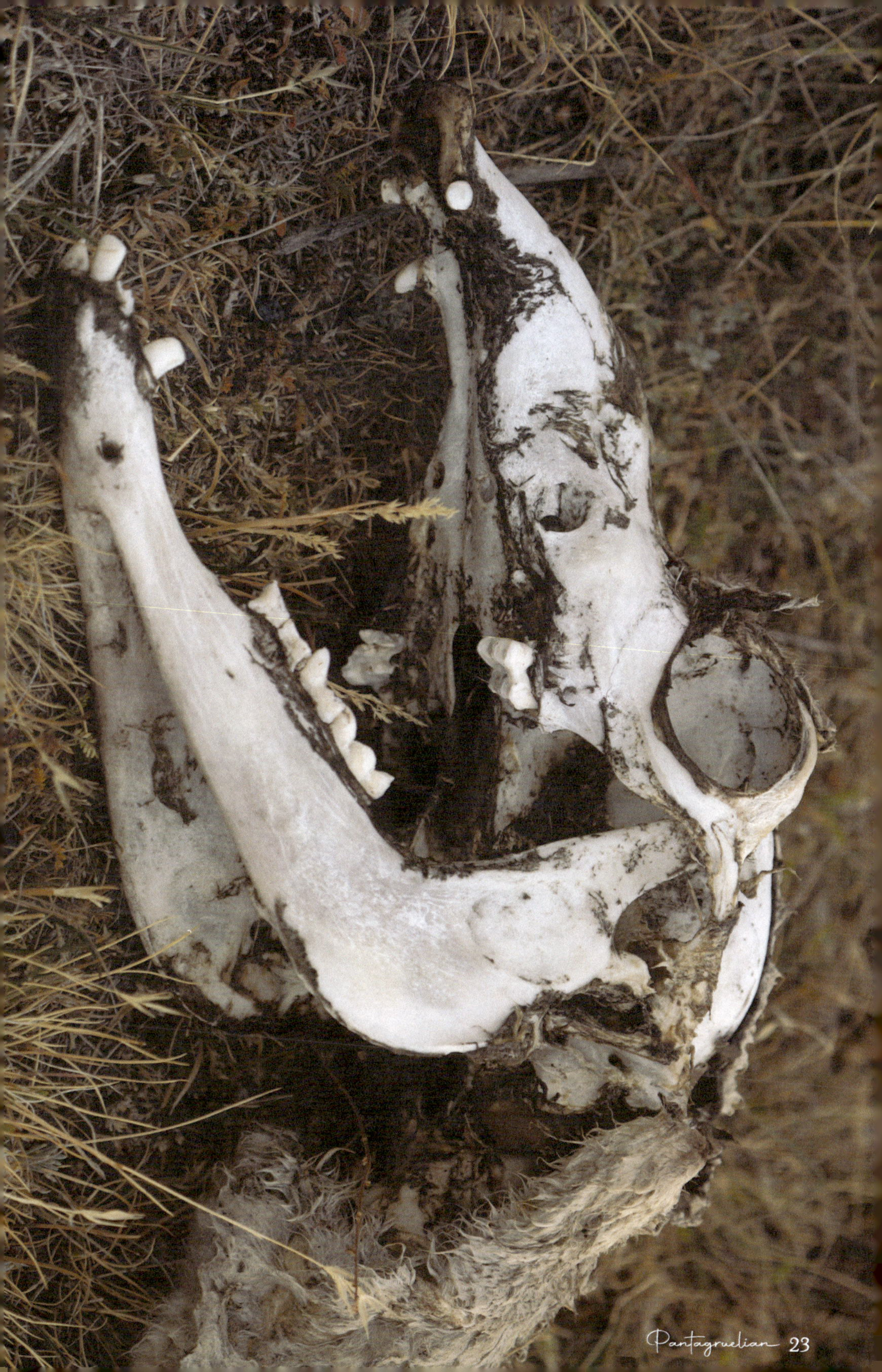
Pantagruelian 23

Andean Condor

At first taint of her, they uplifted.
Catching thermals, priest-condors
Circled. "No, I do not have much time:
Guanaco with leg ensnared,
Yes, guanaco with leg ensnared."
From black lichen rock, they descended.
My distressing cries their cue to cull.
"Bedridden, rotten, I am condemned."

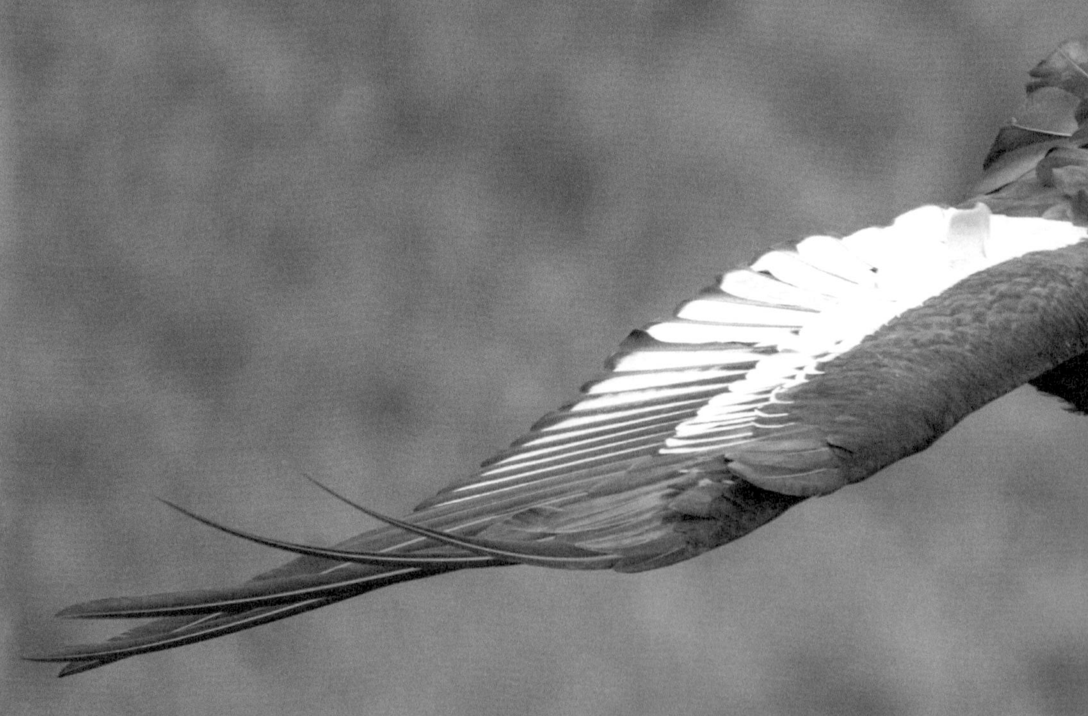

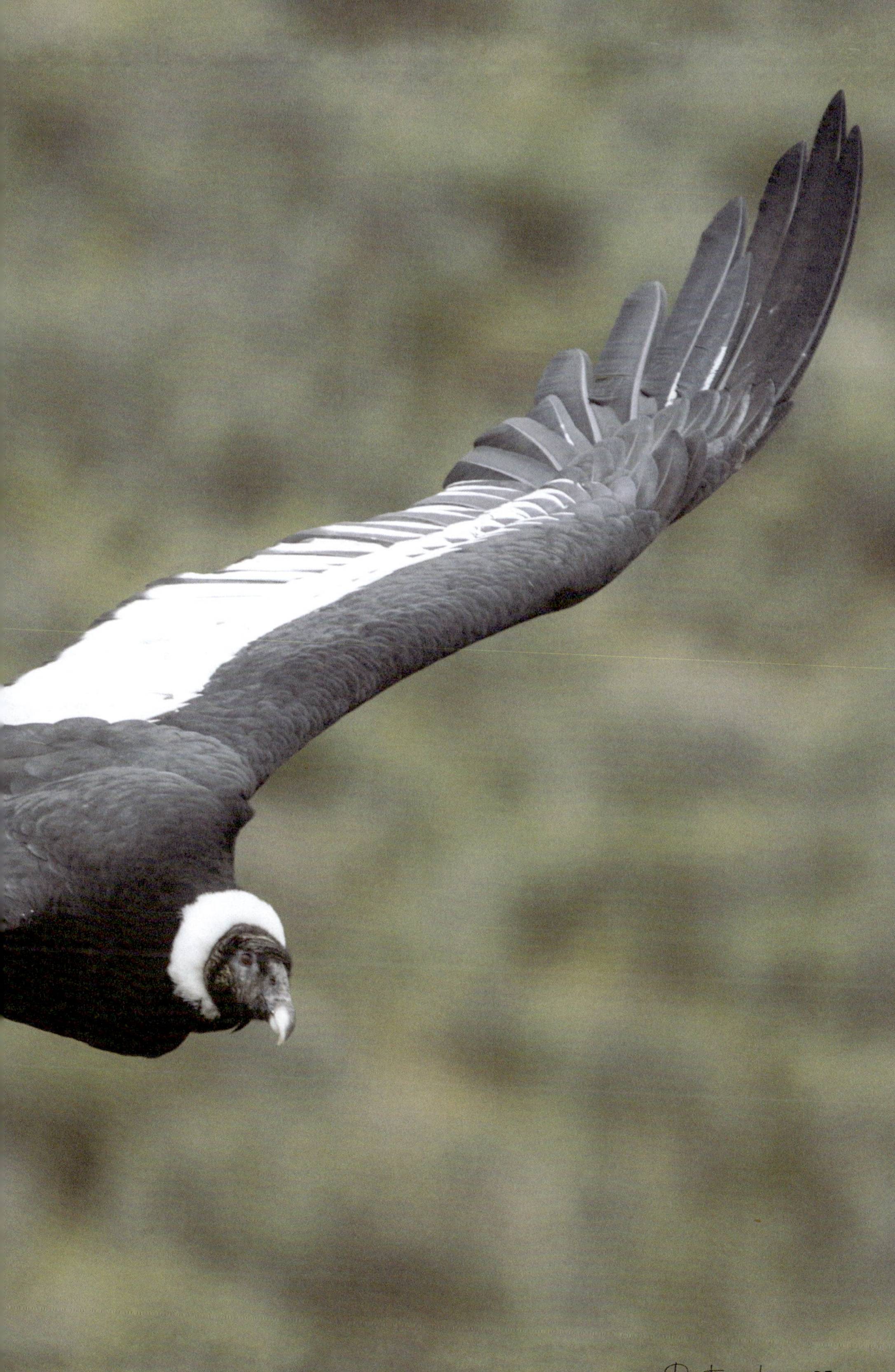
Pantagruelian 25

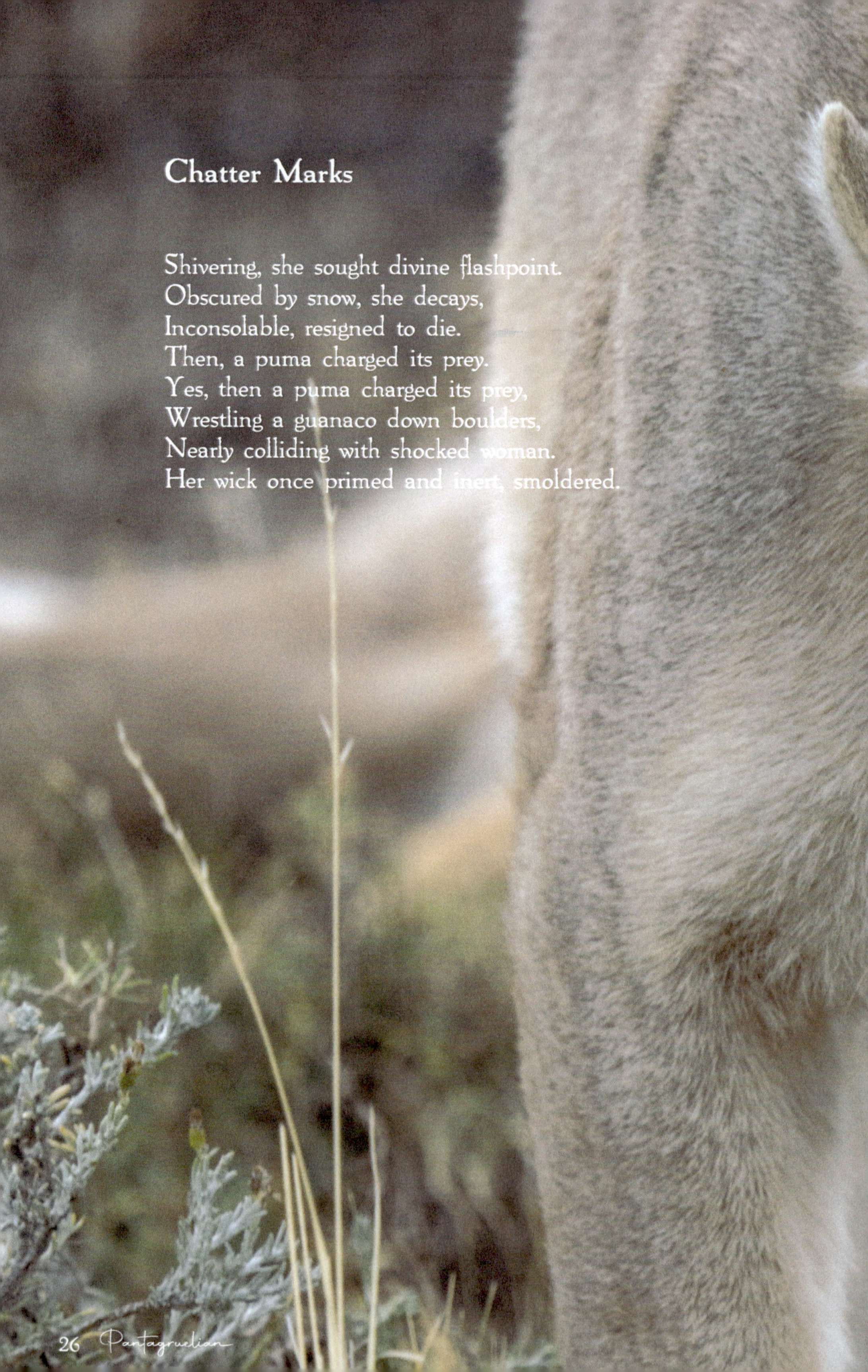

Chatter Marks

Shivering, she sought divine flashpoint.
Obscured by snow, she decays,
Inconsolable, resigned to die.
Then, a puma charged its prey.
Yes, then a puma charged its prey,
Wrestling a guanaco down boulders,
Nearly colliding with shocked woman.
Her wick once primed and inert, smoldered.

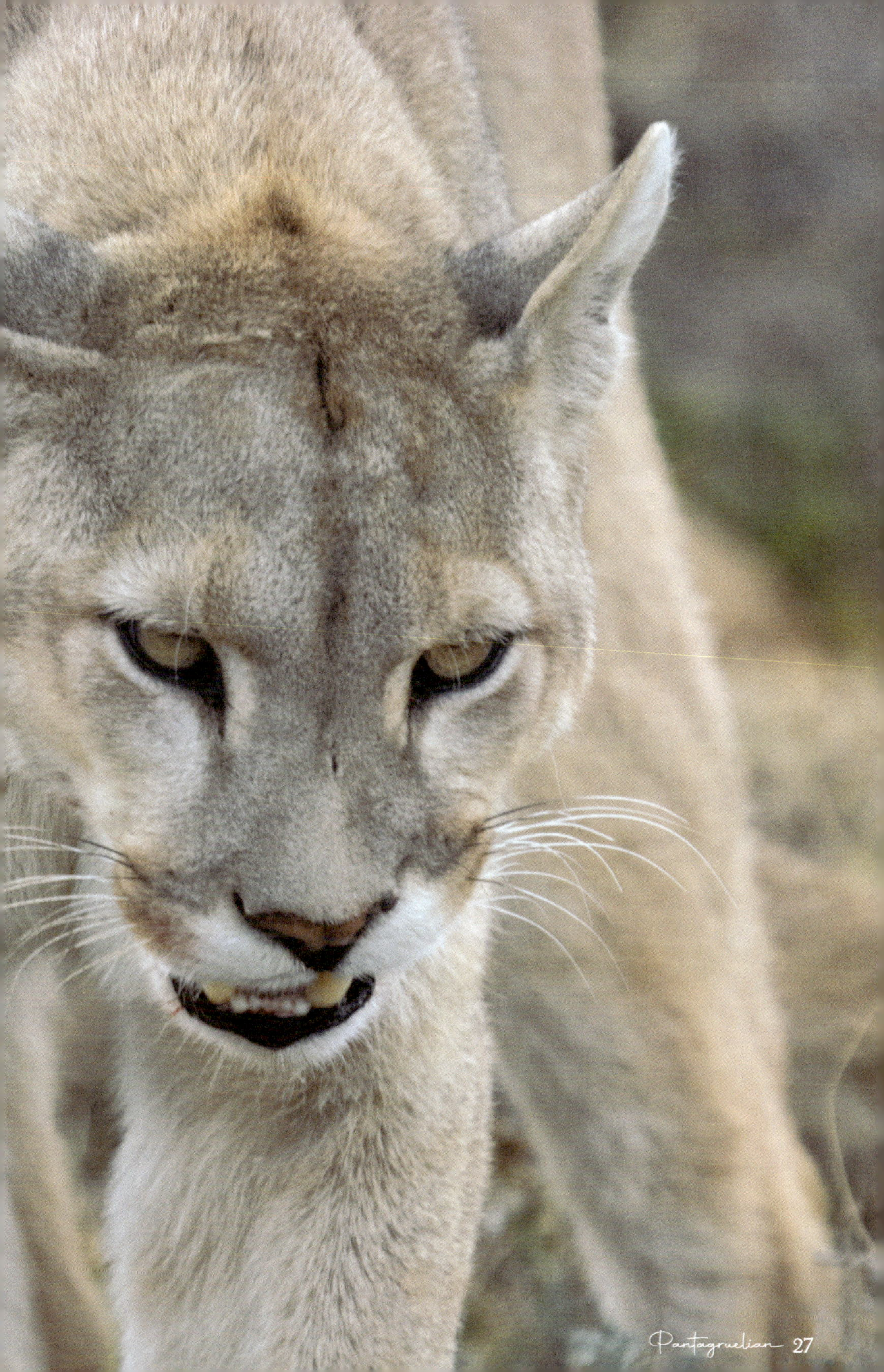

Pantagruelian 27

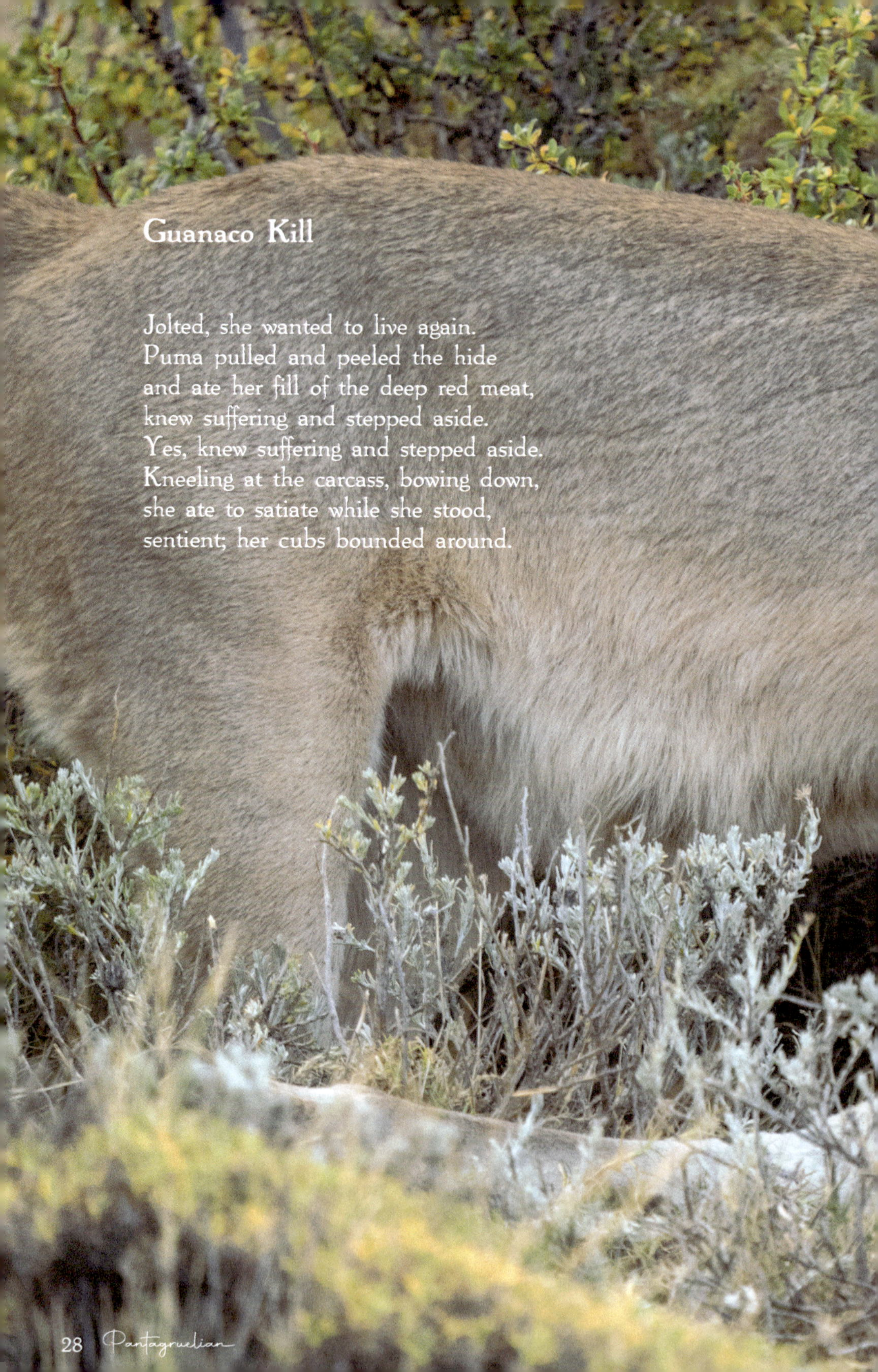

Guanaco Kill

Jolted, she wanted to live again.
Puma pulled and peeled the hide
and ate her fill of the deep red meat,
knew suffering and stepped aside.
Yes, knew suffering and stepped aside.
Kneeling at the carcass, bowing down,
she ate to satiate while she stood,
sentient; her cubs bounded around.

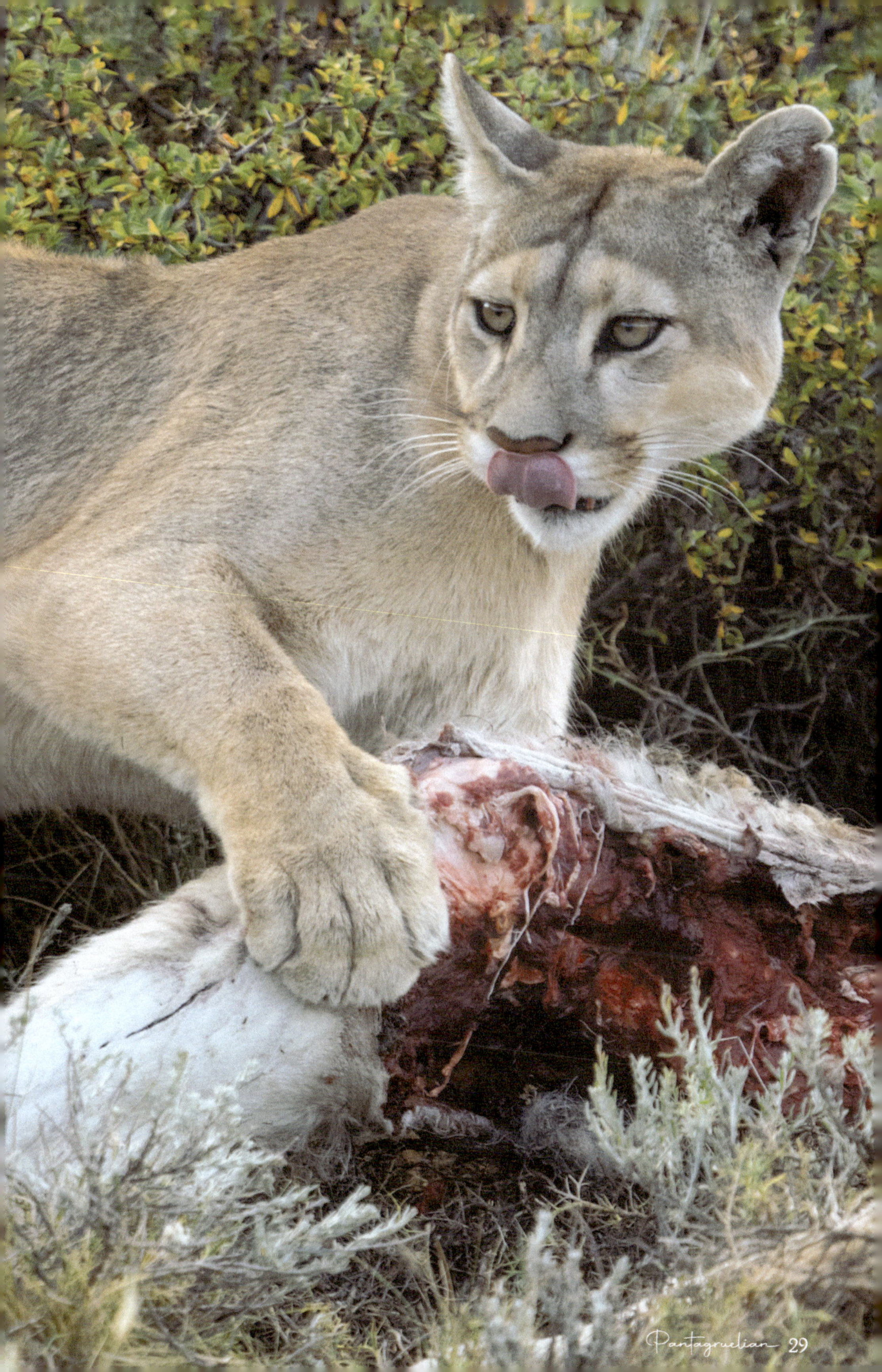
Pantagruelian 29

La Sombra, The Shadow

Her tongue combed her hair and cleaned the blood.
It raked away her despair.
She tended to her, mother to cub.
White whiskers tickled her ear.
Yes, white whiskers tickled her ear.
Her claws napped contently tucked in paws;
Her long tail curled like a treble clef,
Her fur velour, her eyes nebulas.

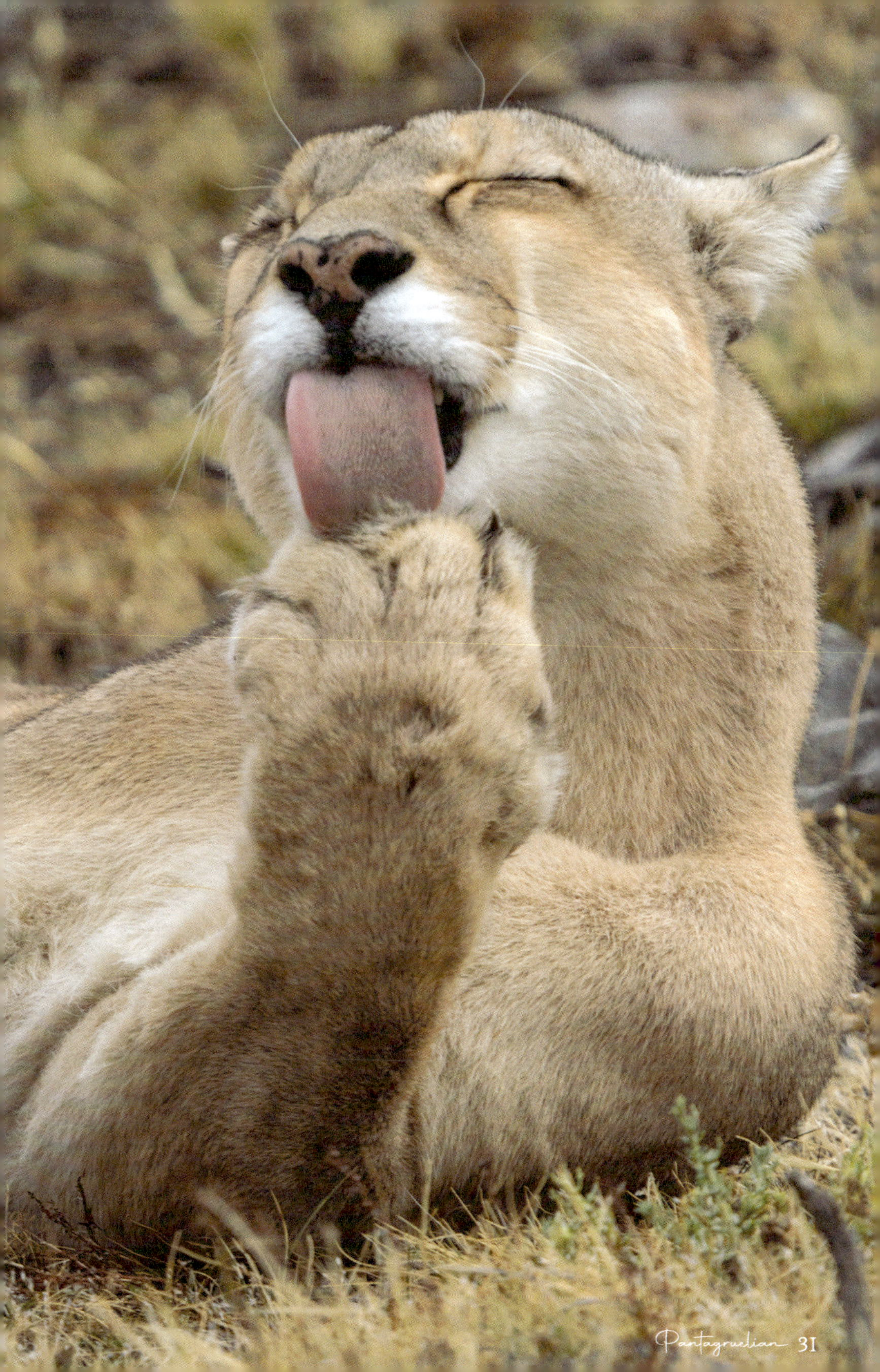
Pantagruelian 31

Torpidity

Benumbed by ten thousand calories
And curled in a cave comatose,
She undulated under thundersnow.
Warm bodies dispersed best dose.
Yes, warm bodies dispersed best dose.
Their throated purrs drowned sound, silencers.
Her atoms vibrated, thrilled children.
She slept, swaddled in sea of fur.

Pantagruelian

Recharged woman was a neutrino,
Weight once zero, trail prolonged
In this universe, pulled from black hole,
Her darkest matter restored.
Yes, her darkest matter restored.
Sunlight traveled straight through her body.
Her gray shadow flipped from strange to charmed.
Her dead forest turned to luscious trees.

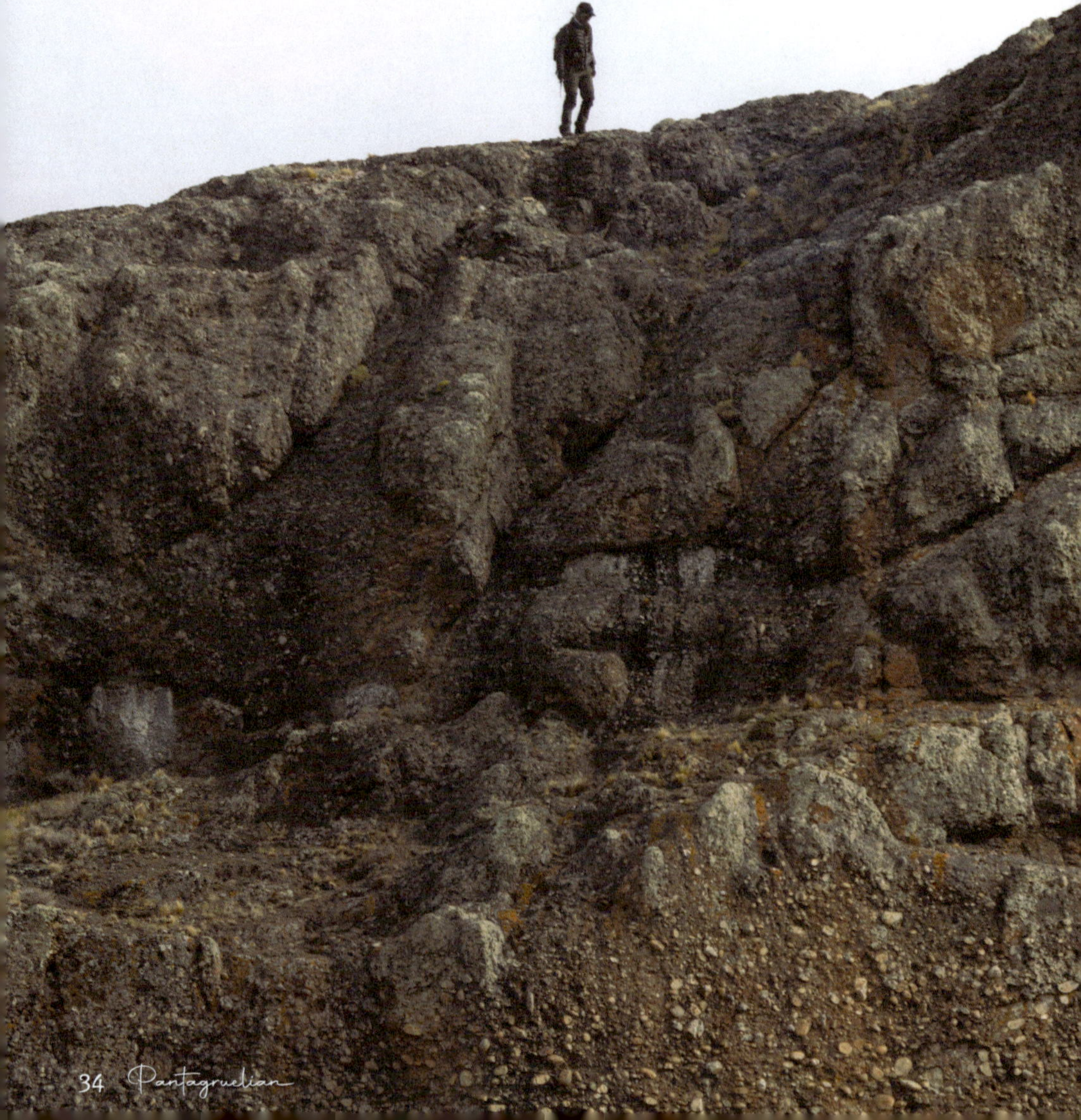

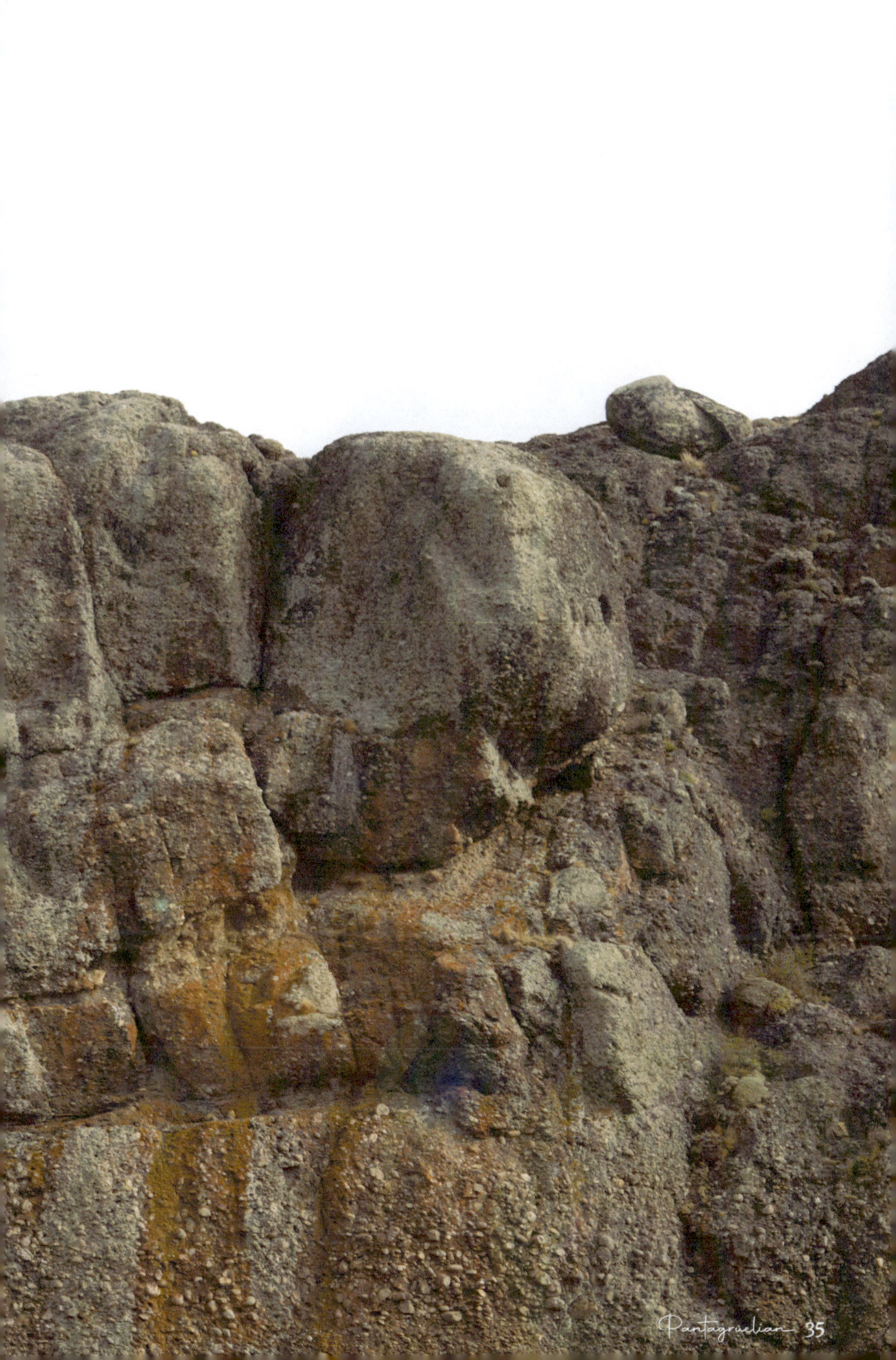
Pantagruelian 35

The Lookout

For decades, she lived quite selfishly.
Here, it was light, food, sleep, trails,
Granite cataracts, orange sandstone,
Protecting cubs from rogue males.
Yes, protecting cubs from rogue males,
Guarding cave's mouth, alert lookout.
The mother chirped and purred in her ear:
Never unwind. Be pure and devout.

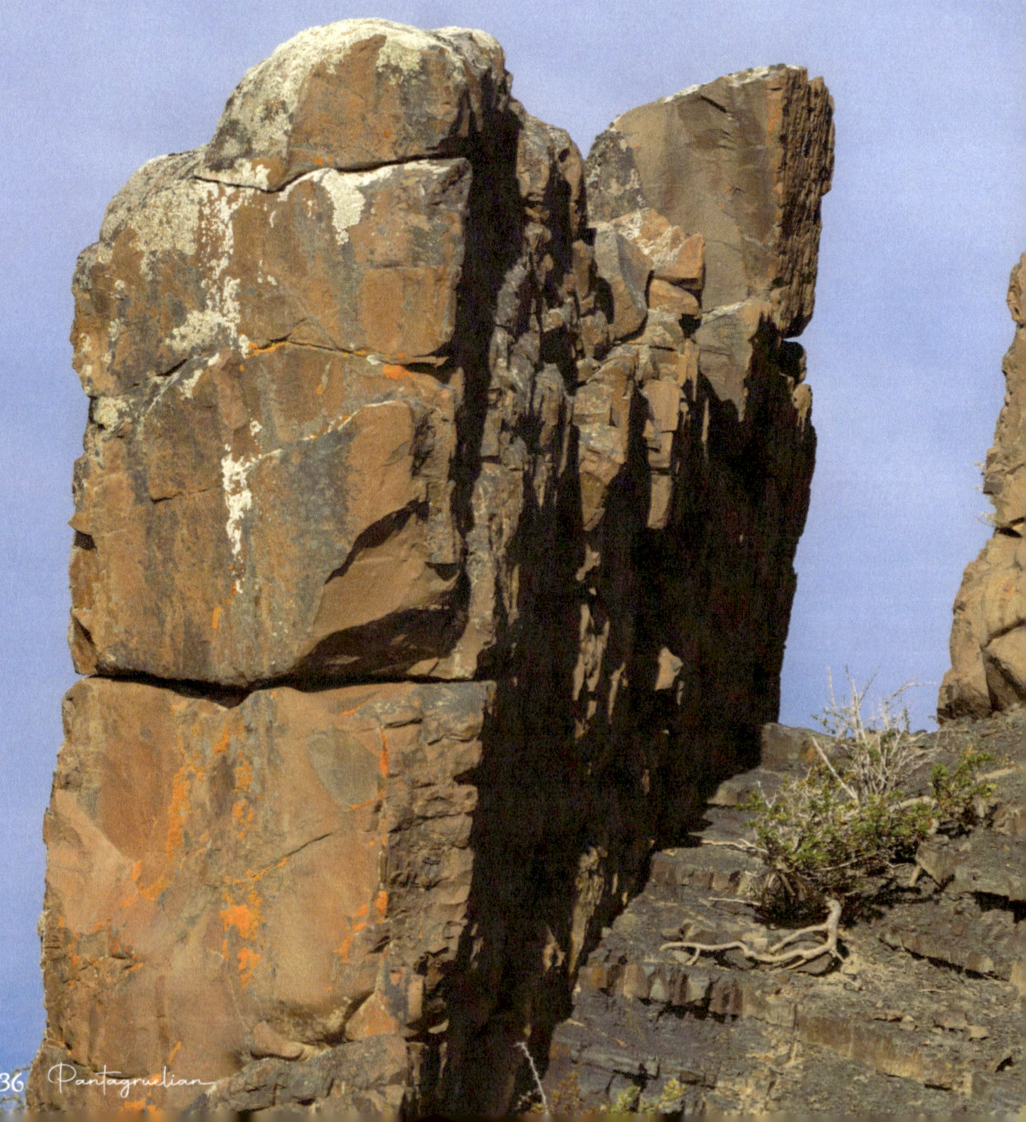

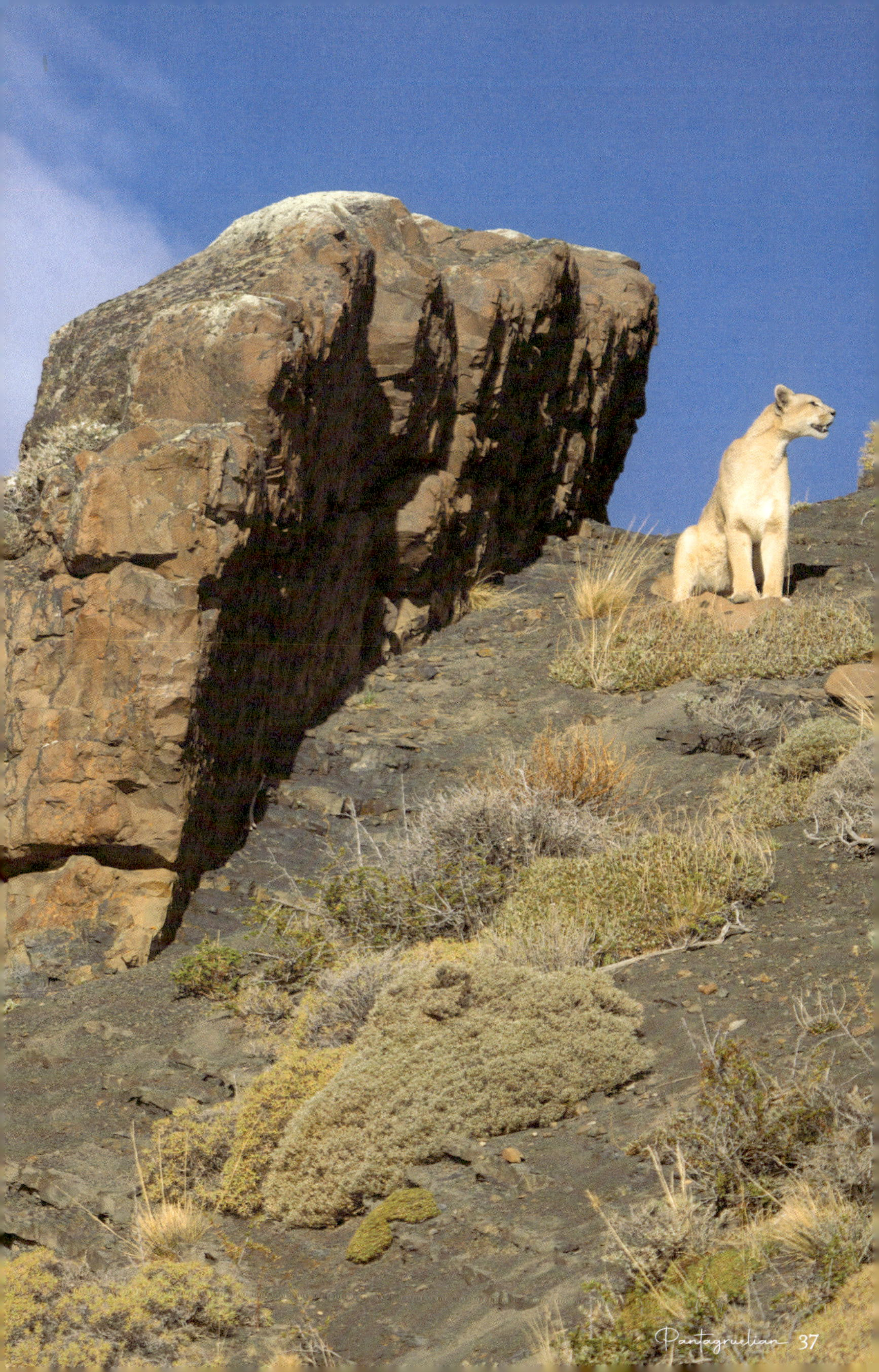
Pantagruelian 37

Reading Prints

Kittens shadowed as she noted prints.
In dry dust, she studied gait,
Width, and the angle between the toes.
The burden a bedrock weight.
Yes, the burden a bedrock weight.
Heel pad huge, angle five degrees more.
Male traced her tracks as she missed a hare,
Stalked a guanaco, drank at the shore.

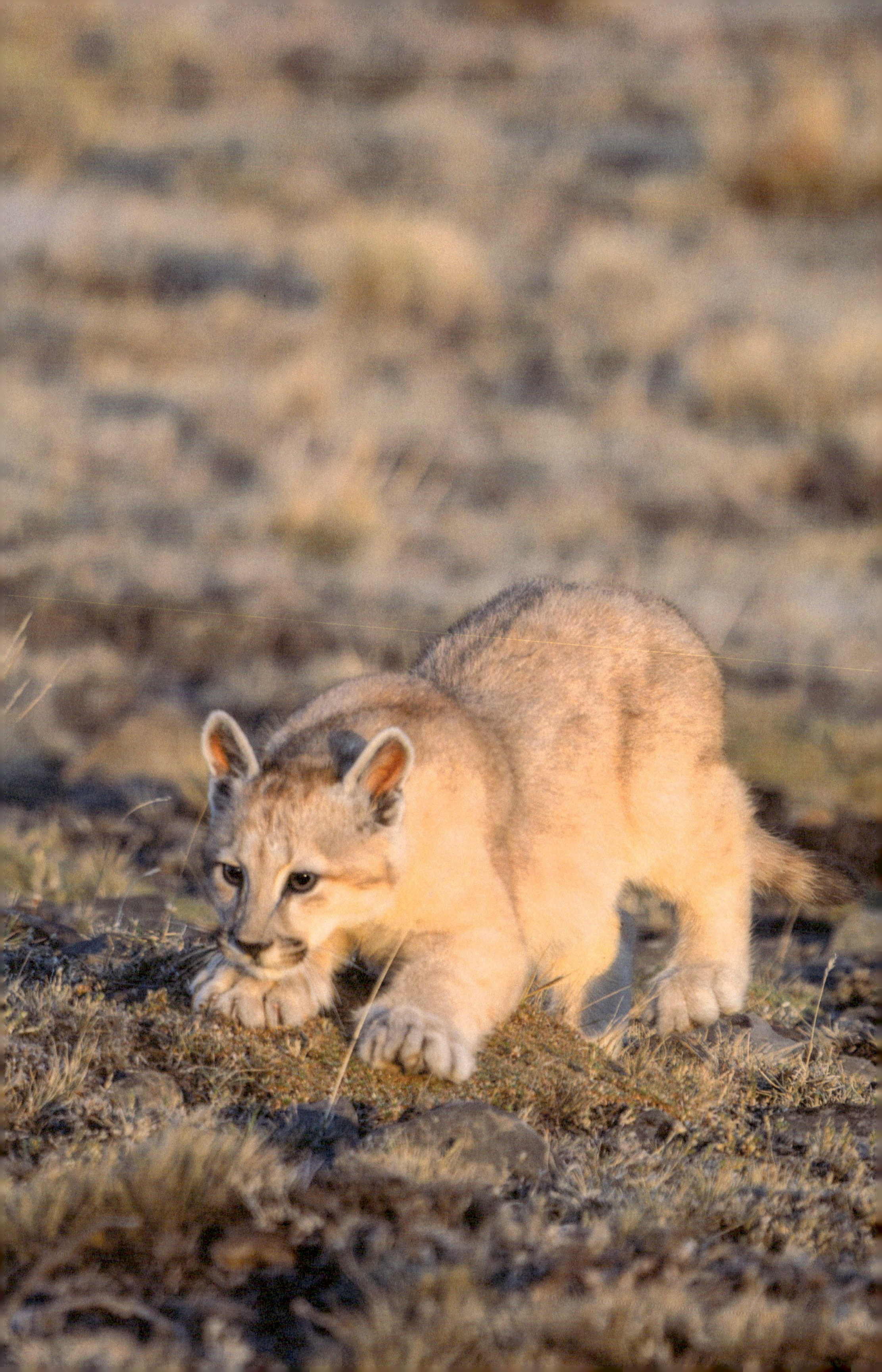

Chulengo

Mortality was greatest in males,
Those not trained by family.
Less social means more fatality.
Attack the periphery.
Yes, attack the periphery.
The naïve are the most vulnerable,
Those with dulled senses at afterlight;
Those detached are most exploitable.

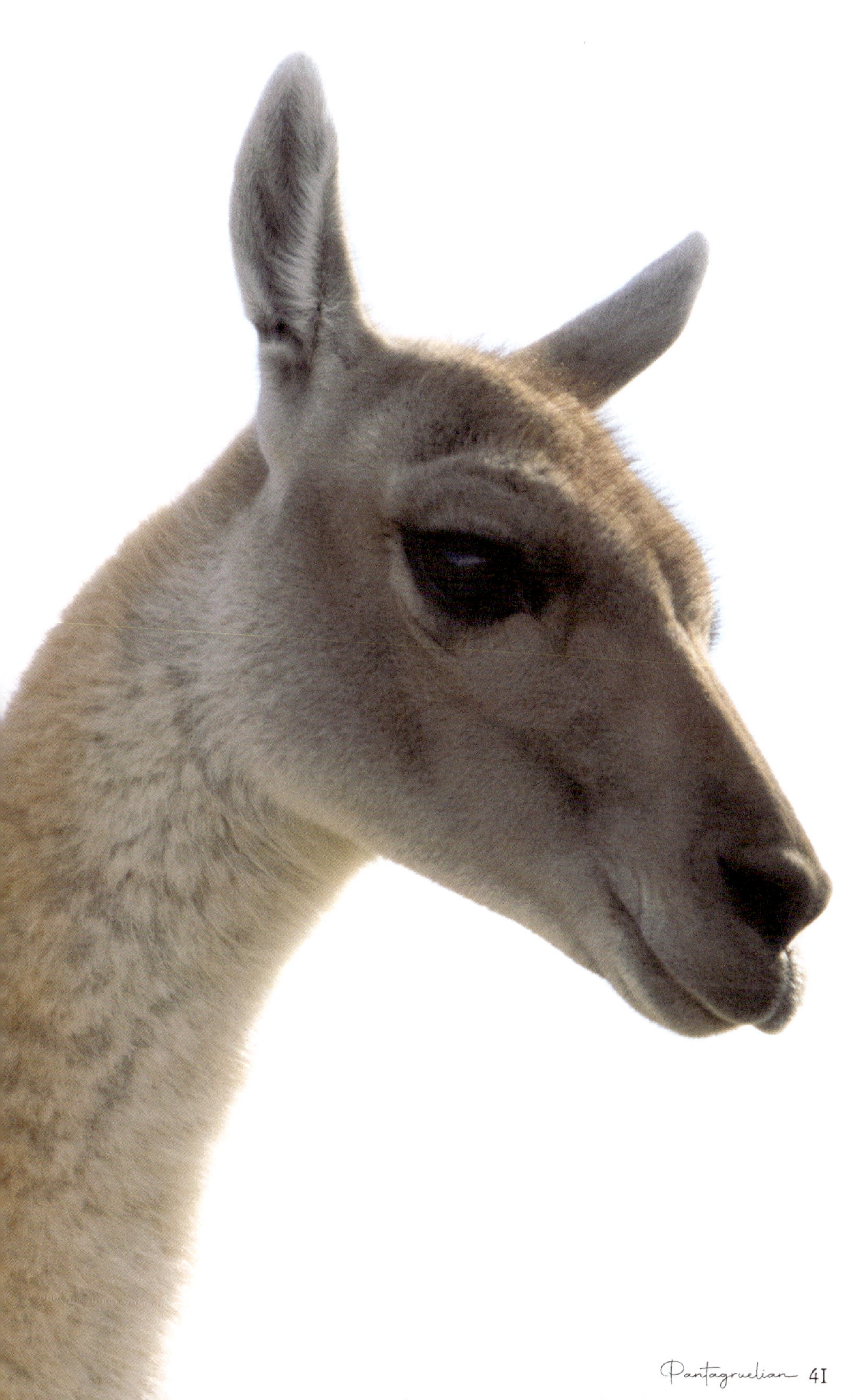
Pantagruelian 41

Salvadora

"We three steered clear of poachers' rifles,
Scorpions, glacial rivers,
Steep cliffs to secure our survival.
Without guidance, they would starve.
Yes, without guidance, they would starve."
Their mother had not returned for days.
She presumed her injured or worse: dead.
These cubs were totally hers to raise.

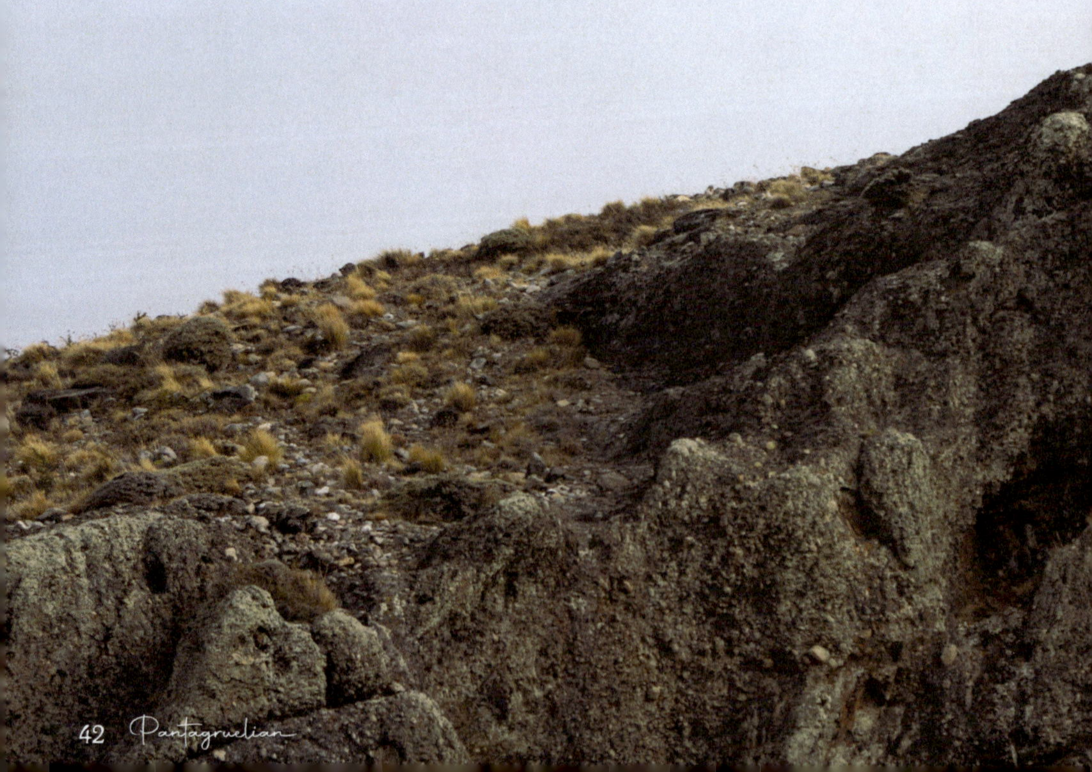

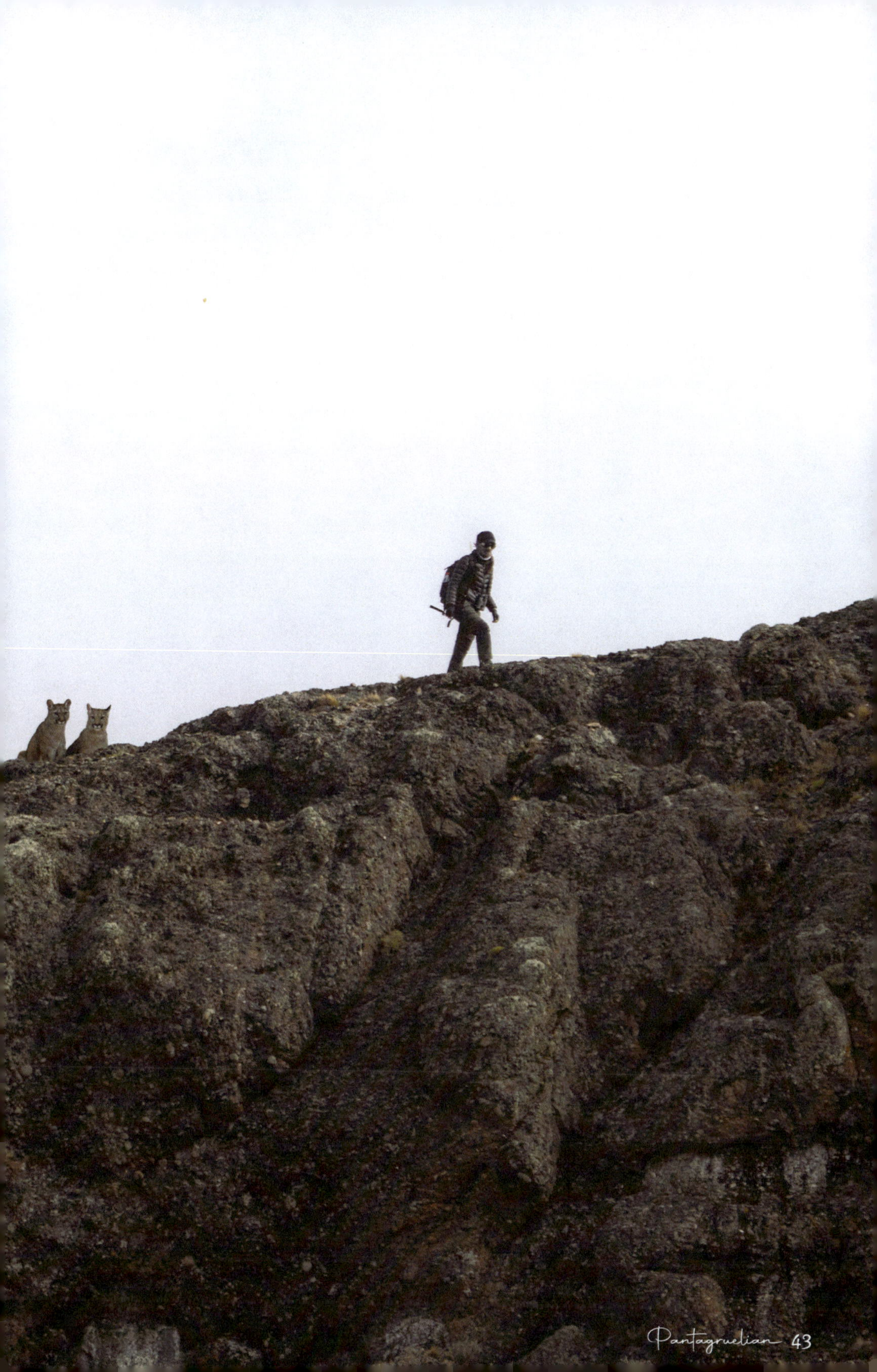
Pantagruelian 43

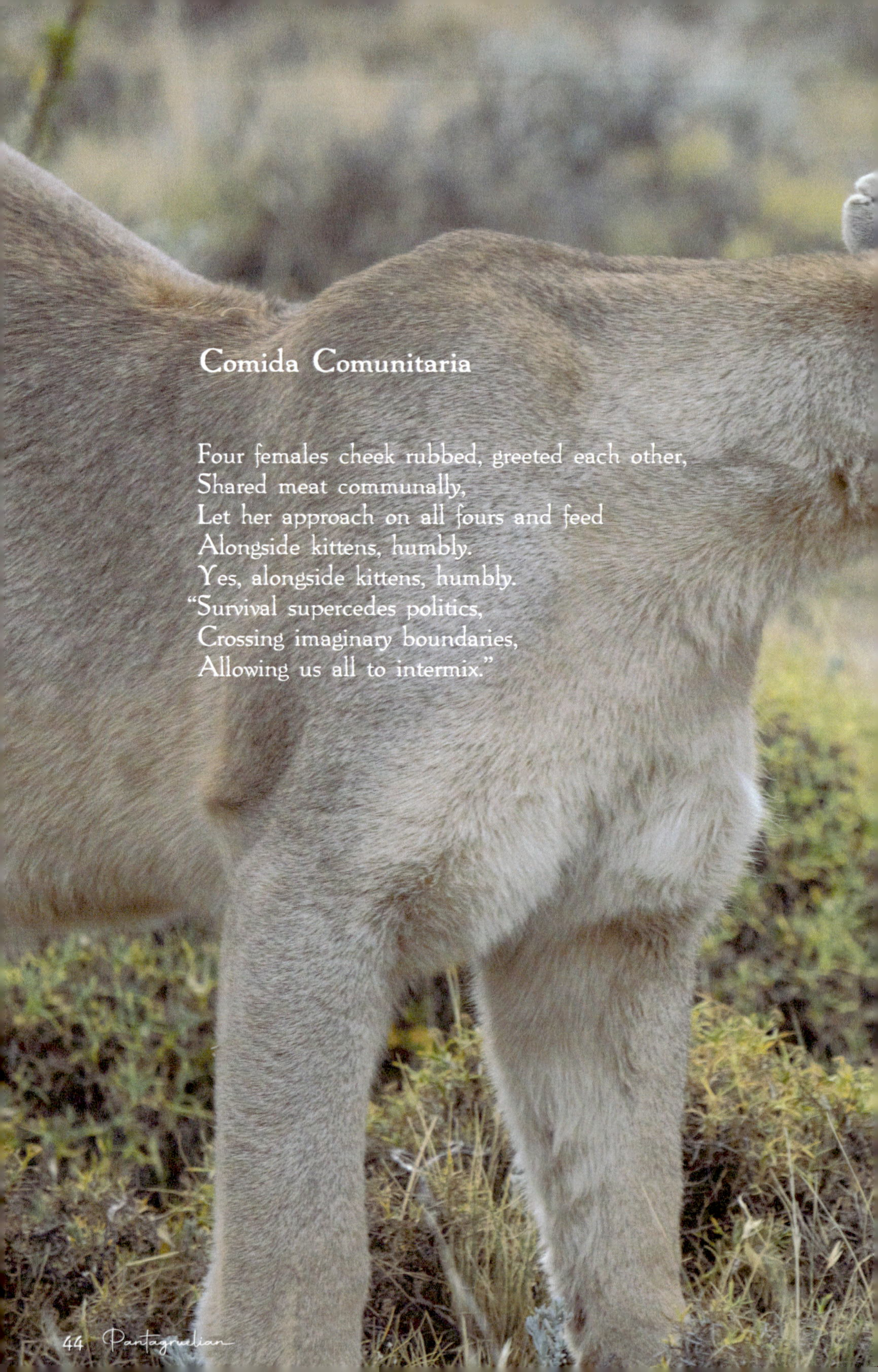

Comida Comunitaria

Four females cheek rubbed, greeted each other,
Shared meat communally,
Let her approach on all fours and feed
Alongside kittens, humbly.
Yes, alongside kittens, humbly.
"Survival supercedes politics,
Crossing imaginary boundaries,
Allowing us all to intermix."

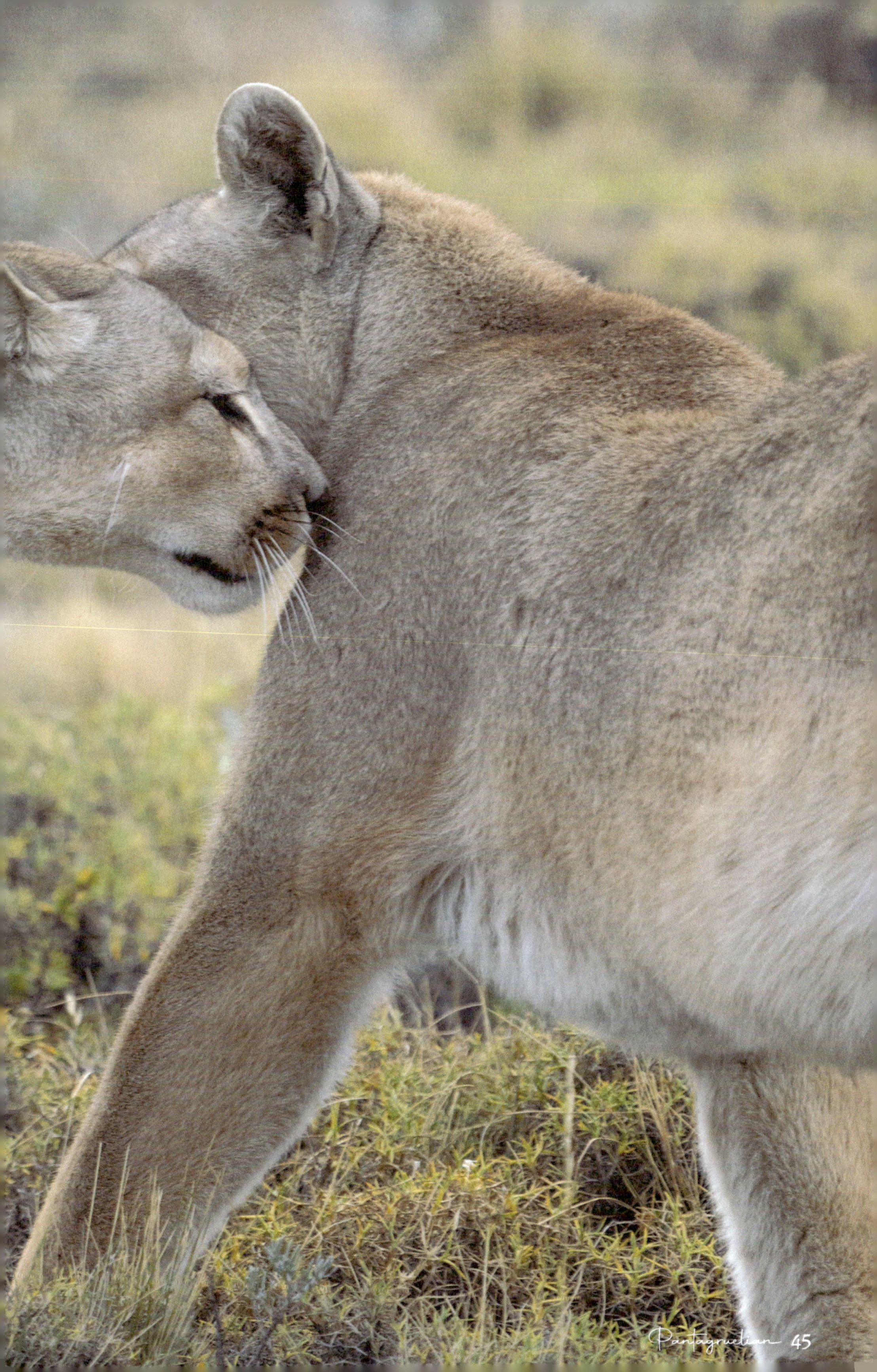
Pantagruelion 45

Supplicant

Her form was lower than theirs, flattened.
Eyes downcast and averted.
Their stomachs distended and fattened.
"We see the wild inverted.
Yes, we see the wild inverted.
I believe in brutal purity,
Not tyranny or dictatorship,
but living authenthically."

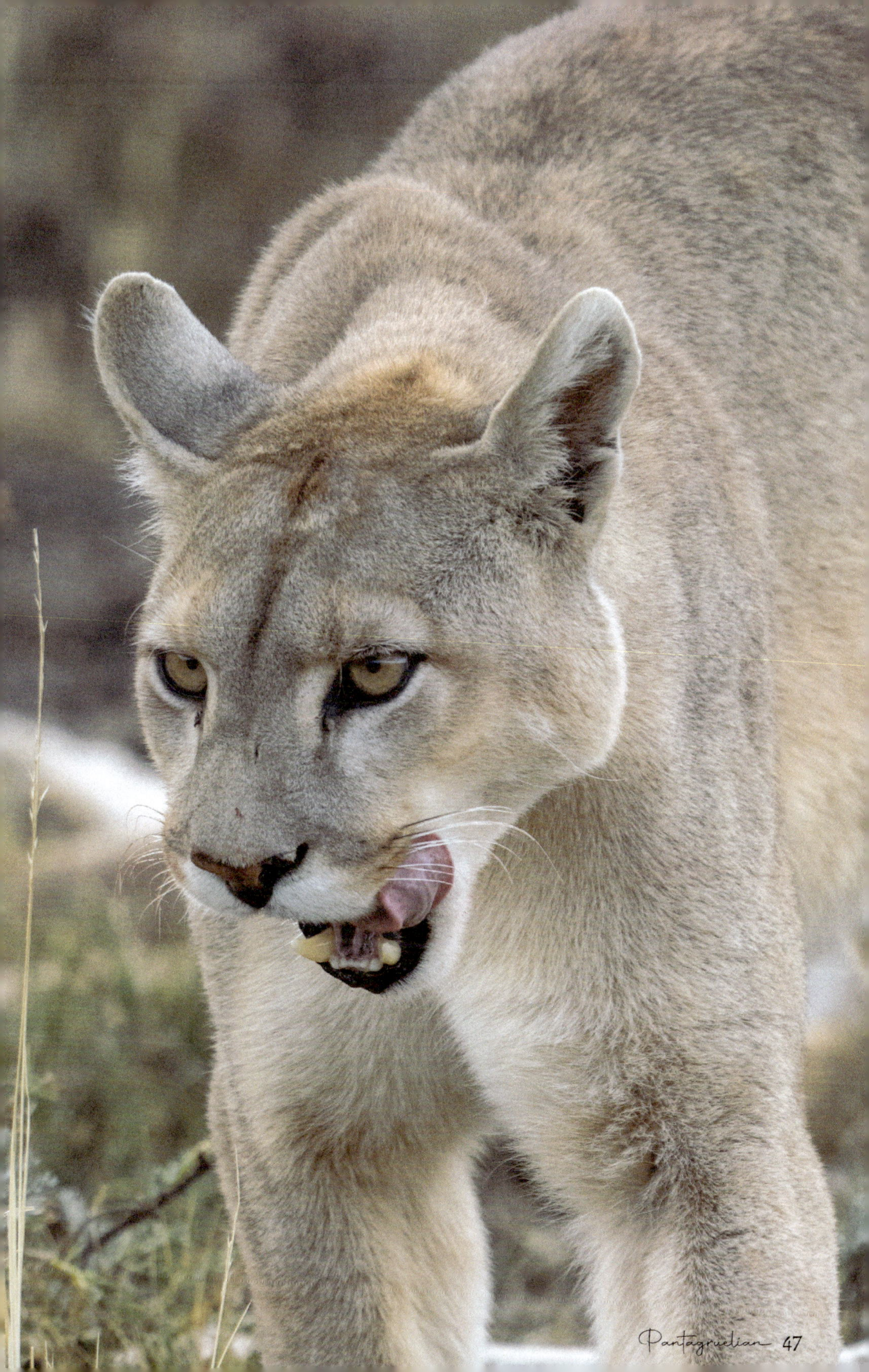
Pantagruelian 47

The Necessity of Play

She'd forgotten the necessity
Of play, rambunctious outrage,
Shenanigans as they nipped her ears.
"Play recalibrates old age.
Yes, play recalibrates old age":
Stalk and tackle, wrangle, mock battle.
Quick skedaddle, straddle, zoom and groom,
Cuddle, fake guanaco neck strangle.

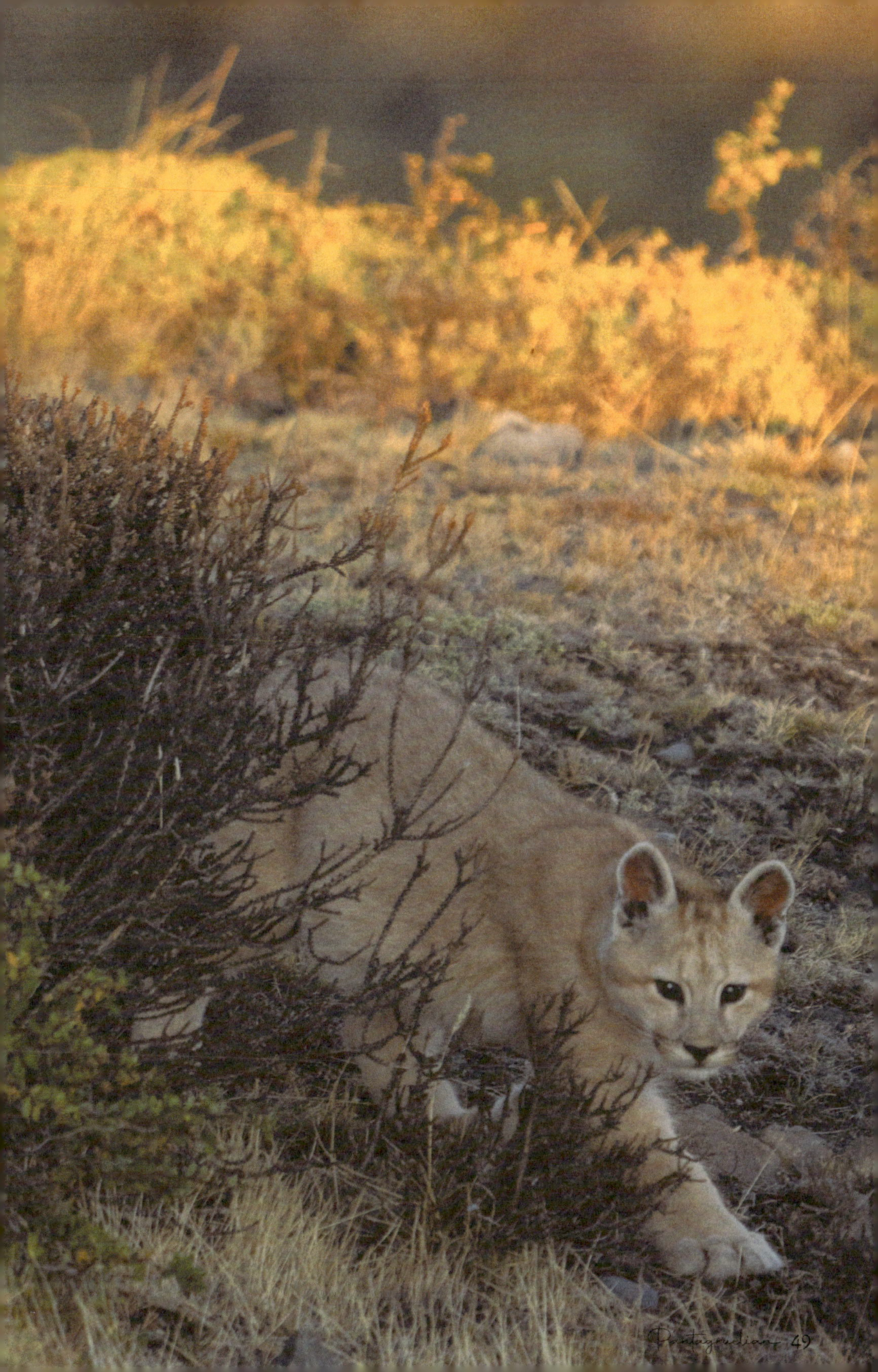

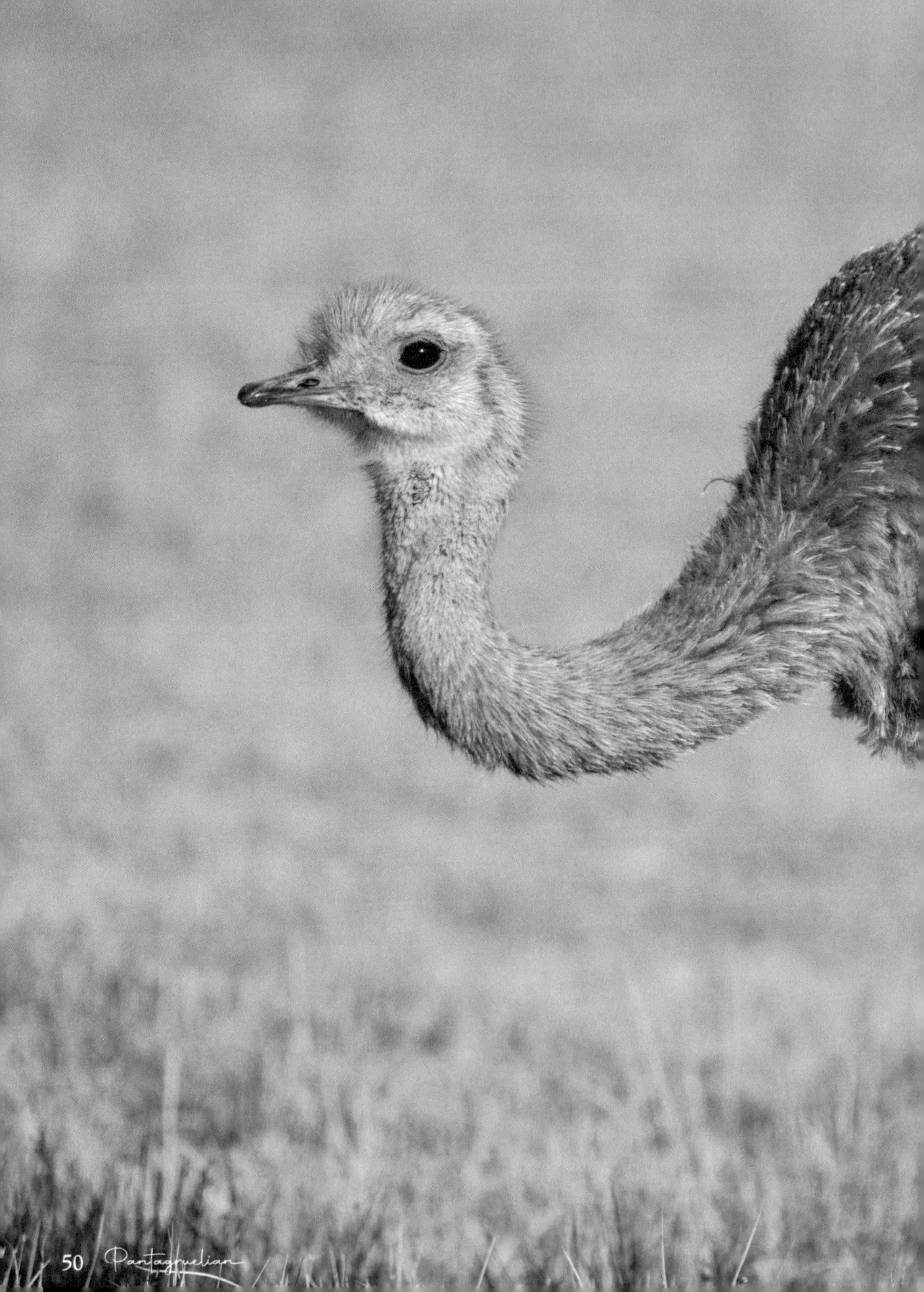

 Pantagruelian

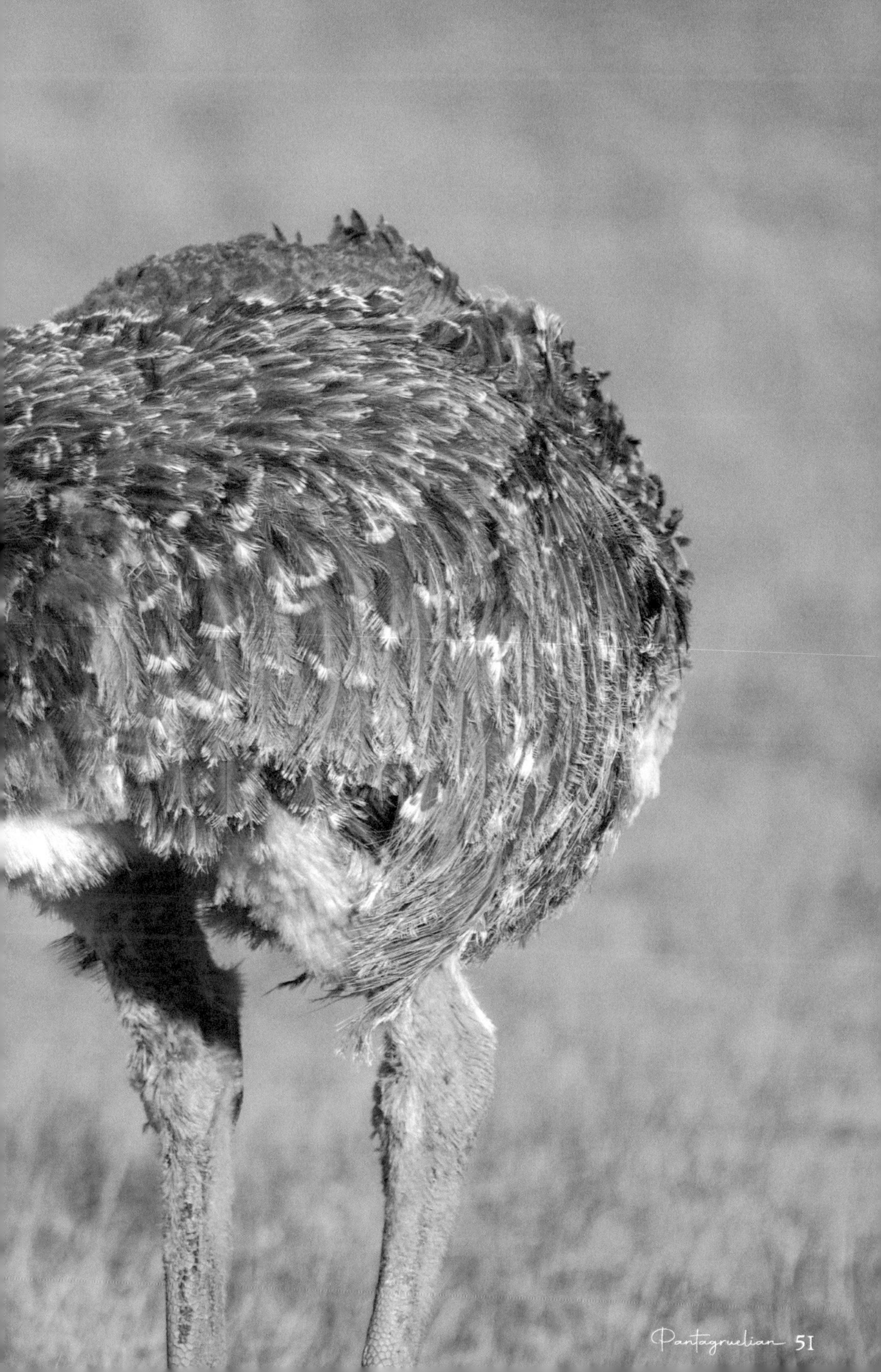
Pantagruelian 51

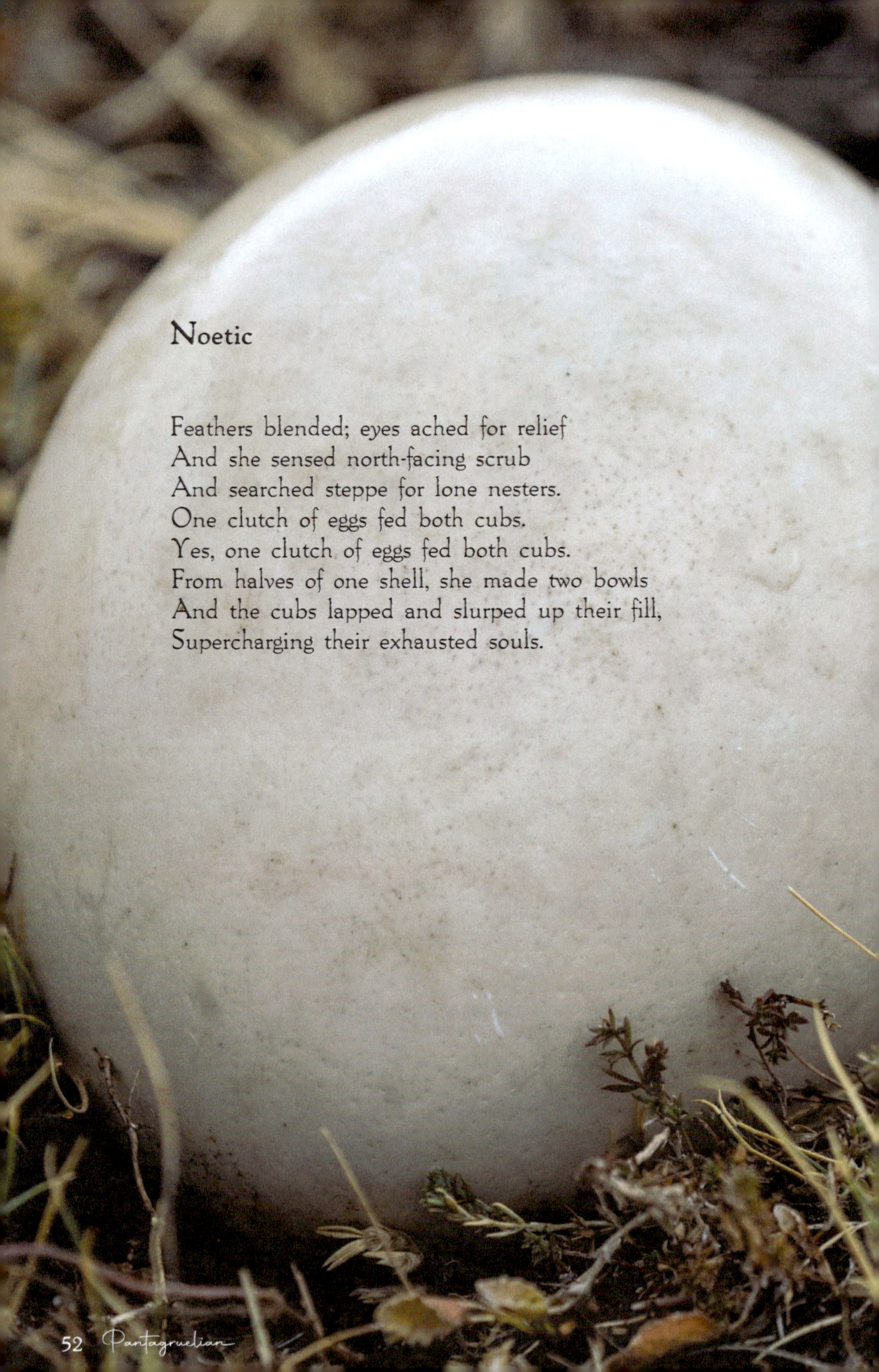

Noetic

Feathers blended; eyes ached for relief
And she sensed north-facing scrub
And searched steppe for lone nesters.
One clutch of eggs fed both cubs.
Yes, one clutch of eggs fed both cubs.
From halves of one shell, she made two bowls
And the cubs lapped and slurped up their fill,
Supercharging their exhausted souls.

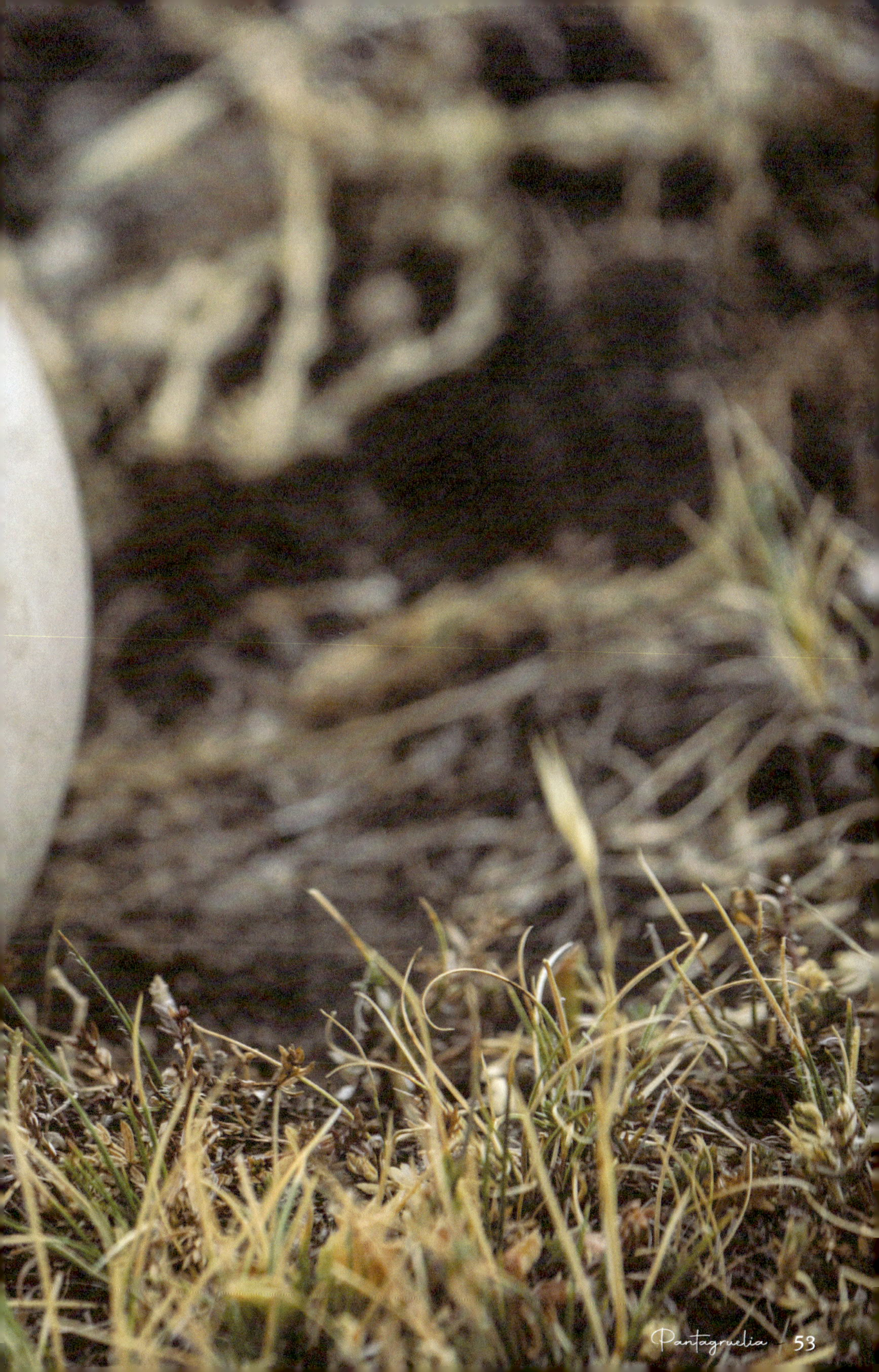
Pantagruelia 53

Zorro Chilla

Swiftly, predator dissolved to prey
And knew well to be afraid.
In only seven generations,
Foxes can be handraised, tamed.
Yes, foxes can be handraised, tamed.
Around large cubs, foxes made wide arcs.
Pumas, arbiters of certain death,
Dominated the hierarchy.

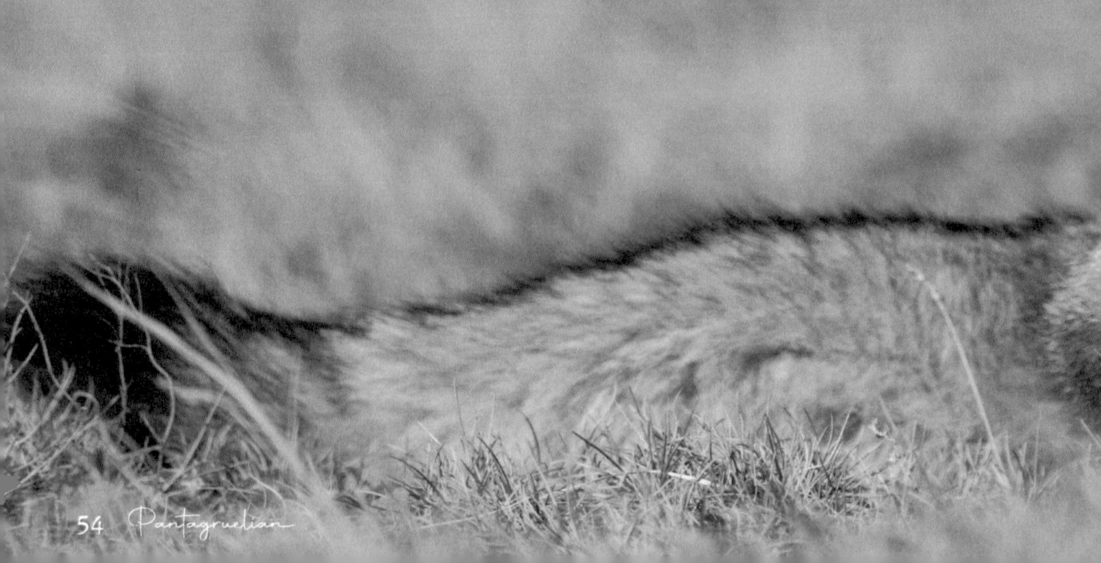

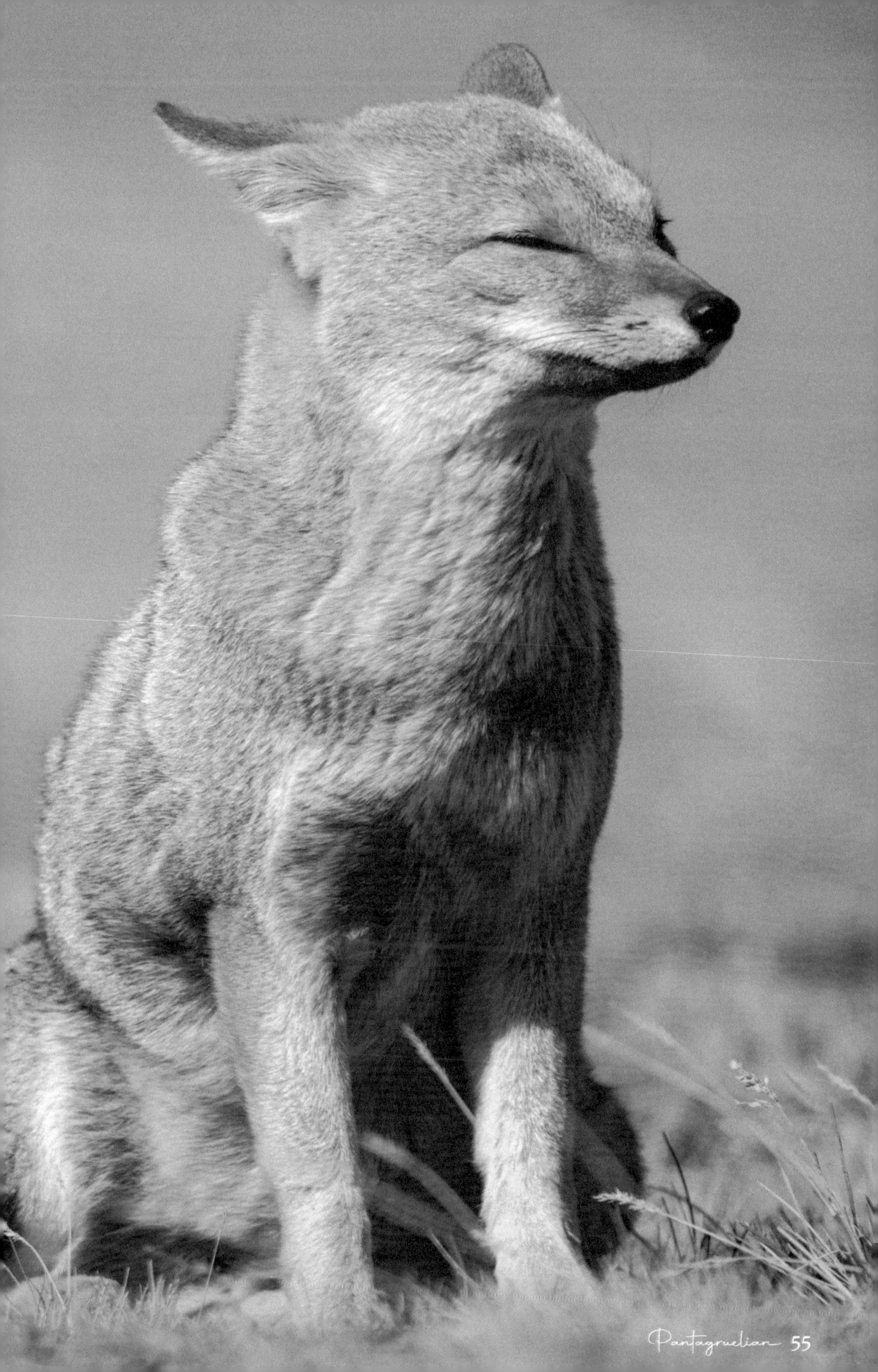
Pantagruelian 55

Valuation

Chingüe teargassed calfate.
She extended a branchlet
And cubs hedged at the vomitous stench.
Thiols were liquid assets.
Yes, thiols were liquid assets,
Allowed for independency,
For upticks on ledger sheet.
Loss meant gains in life expectancy.

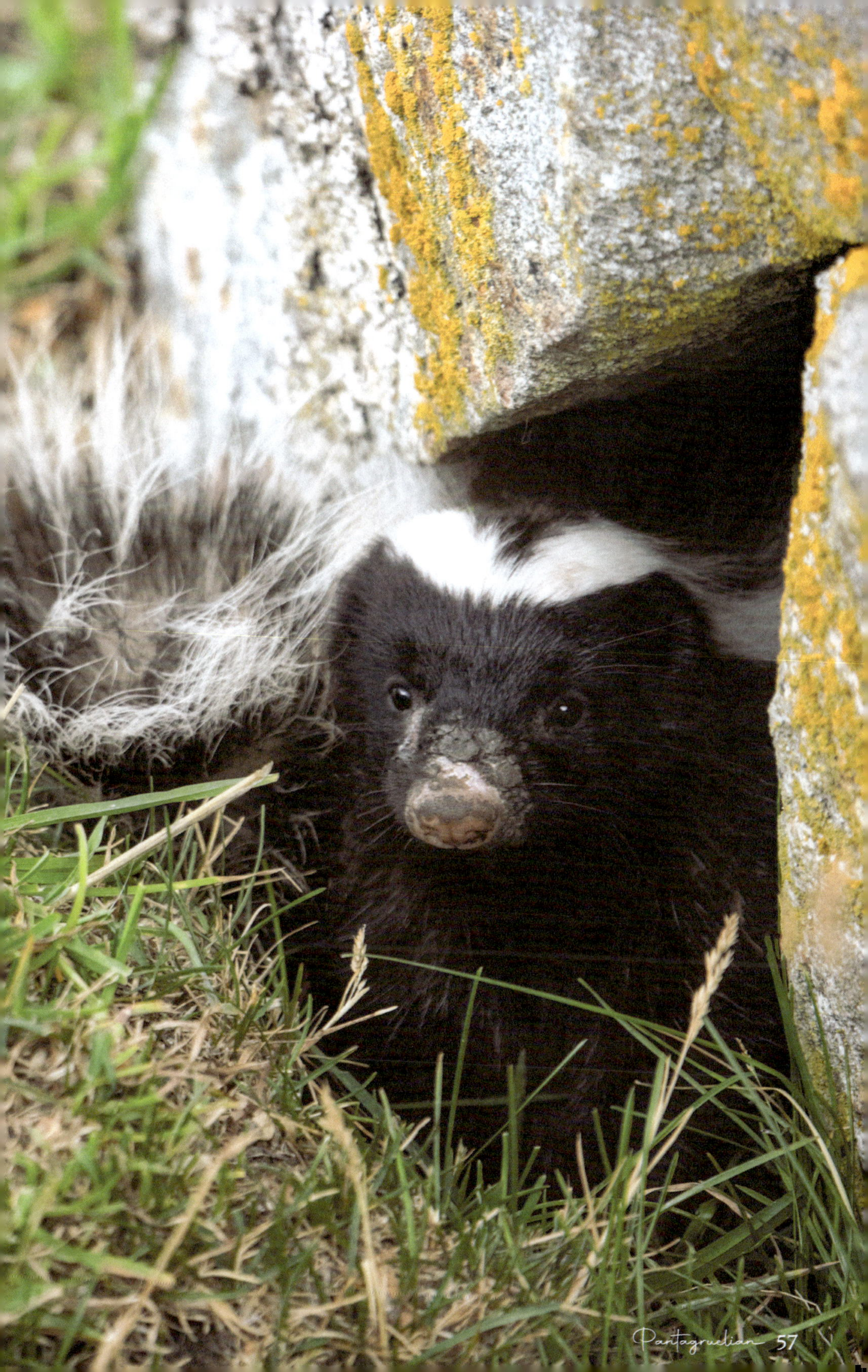
Pantagruelian

Hunter of Lions

Unwanted advances unwelcomed.
Hid cubs in underbellies
Of caves, she kept to rocks to mask tracks.
Cazador de Leones,
Yes, Cazador de Leones
Turned sideways through their disappearance,
Finding only a woman's footprints
And corroding his self-confidence.

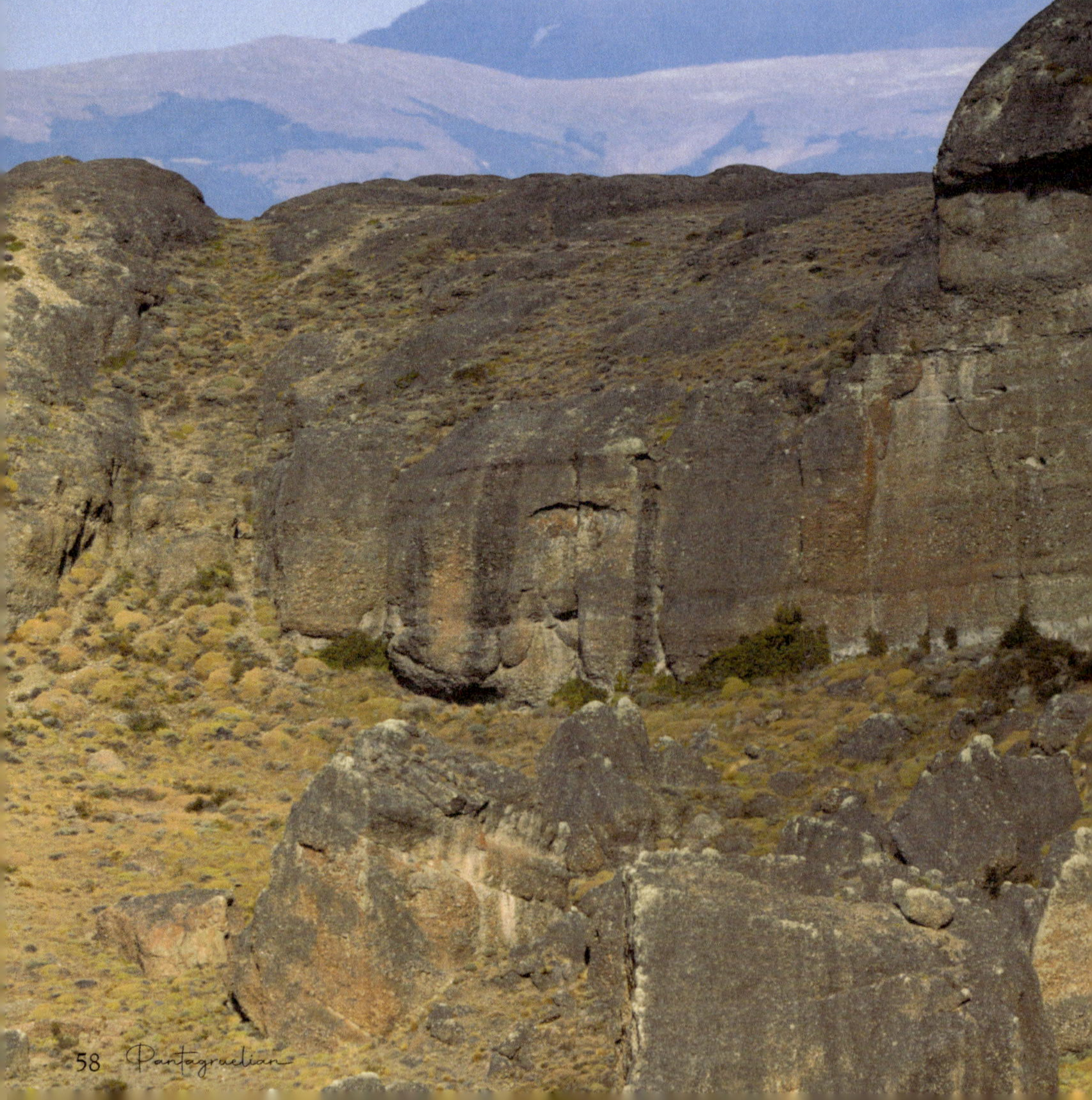

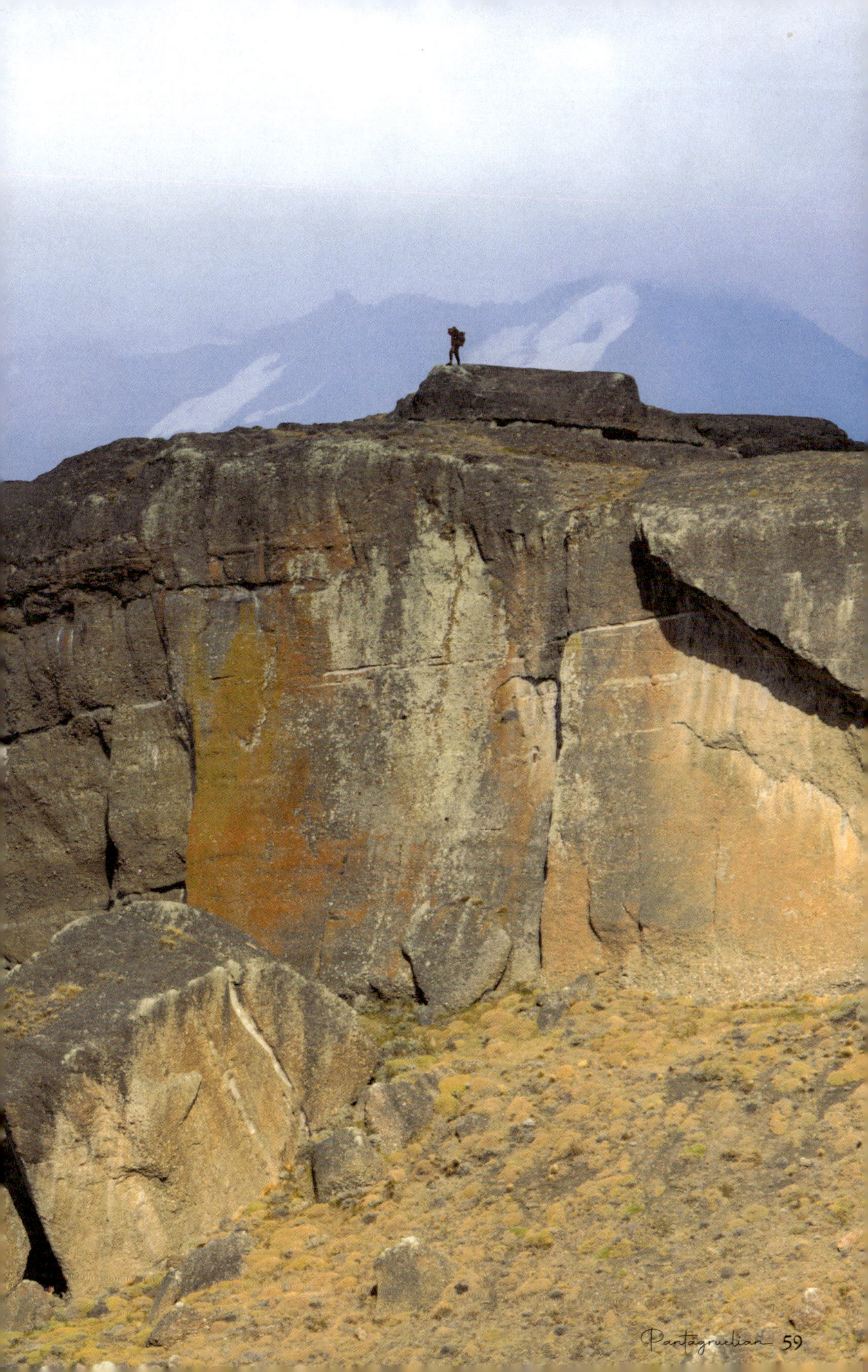

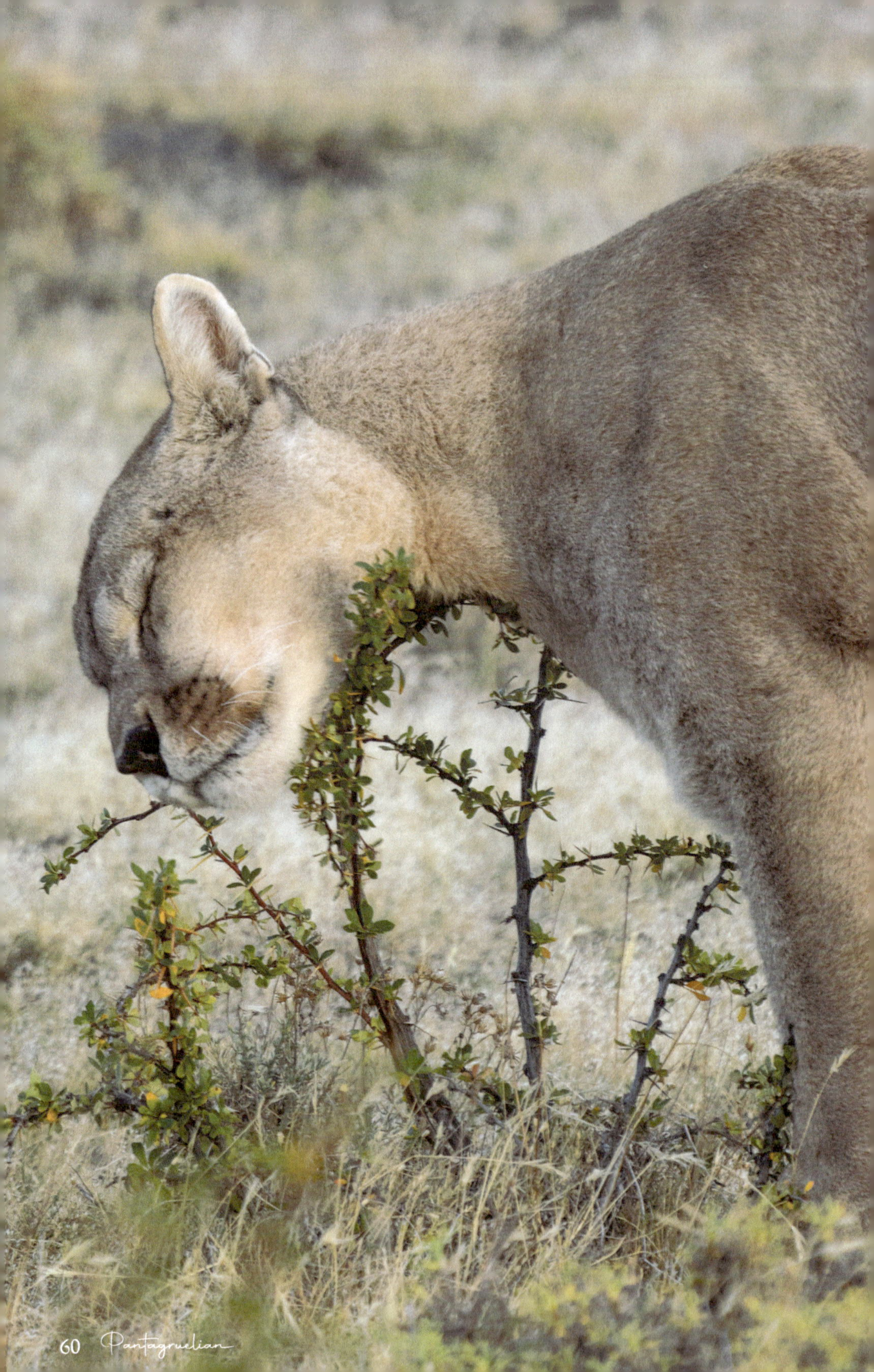

 Pantagruelian

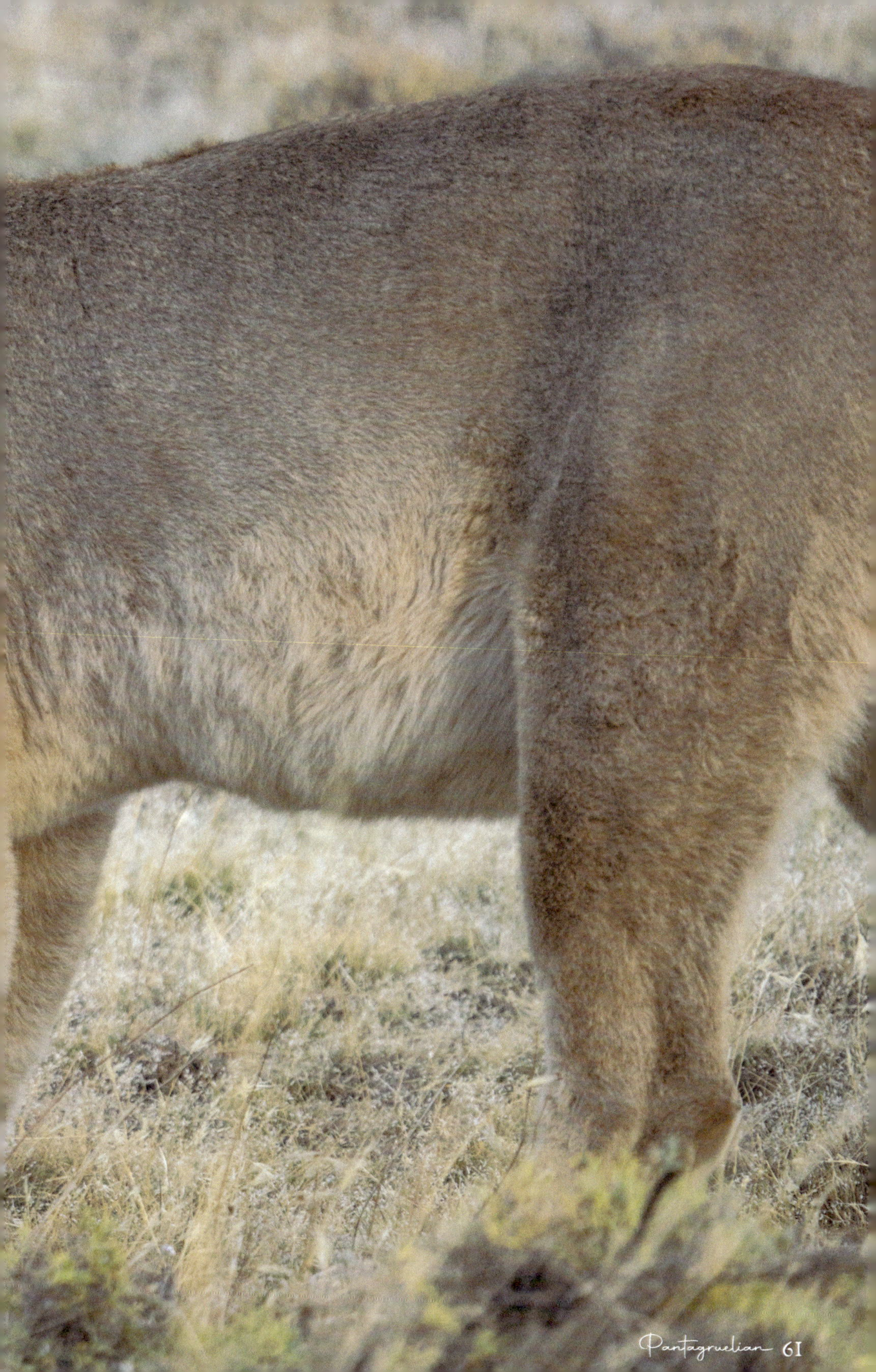
Pantagruelian_ 61

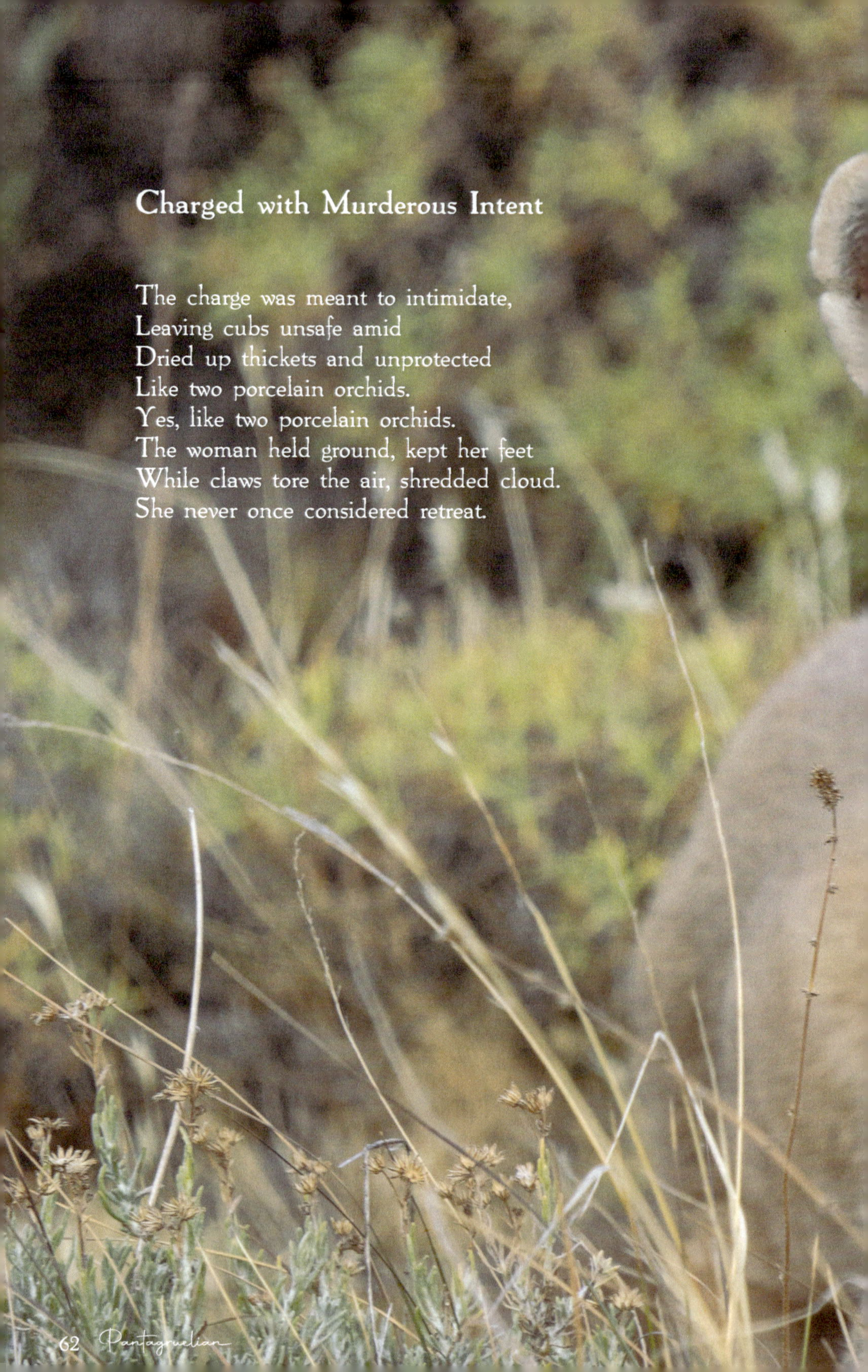

Charged with Murderous Intent

The charge was meant to intimidate,
Leaving cubs unsafe amid
Dried up thickets and unprotected
Like two porcelain orchids.
Yes, like two porcelain orchids.
The woman held ground, kept her feet
While claws tore the air, shredded cloud.
She never once considered retreat.

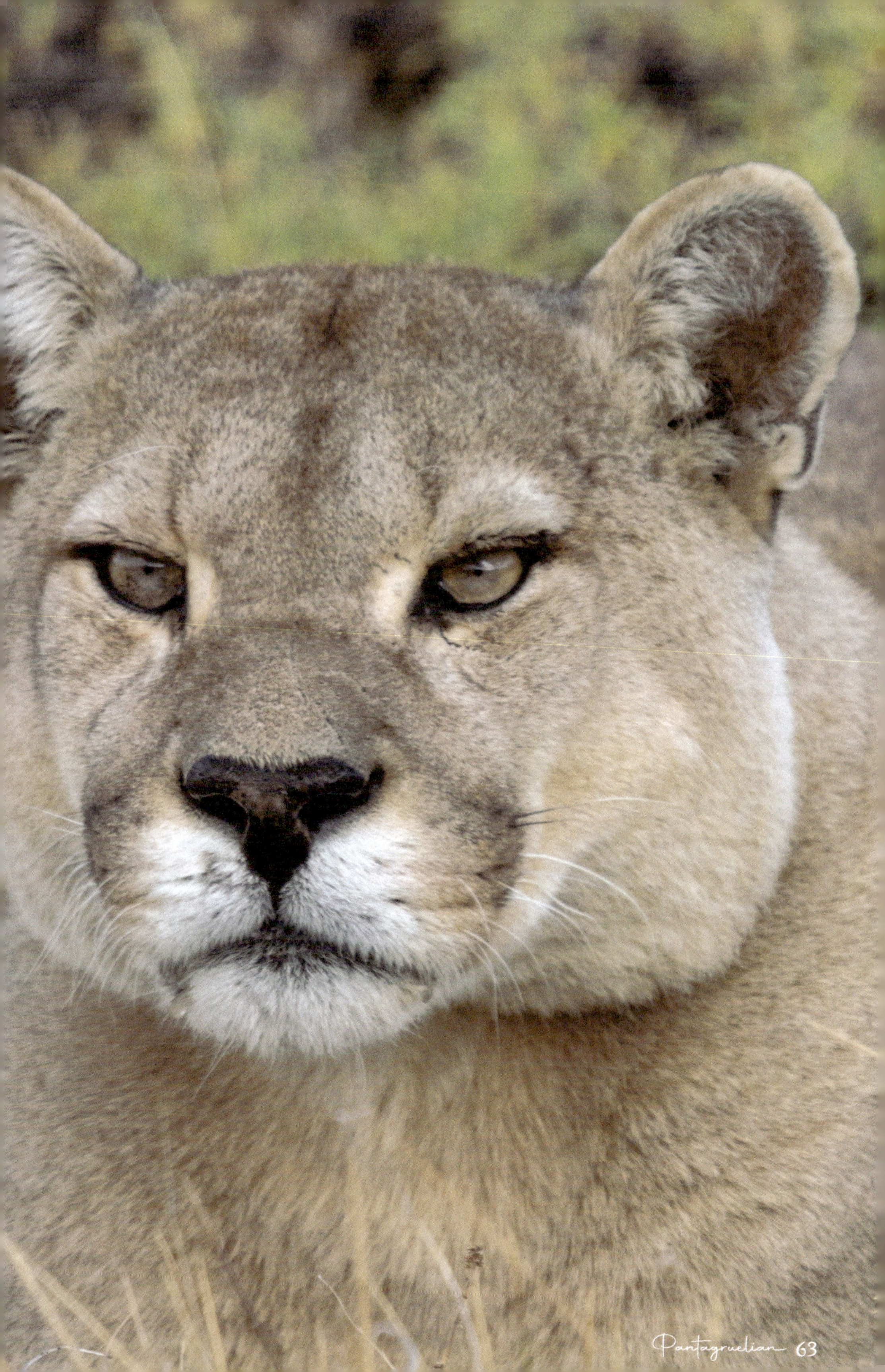
Pantagruelian 63

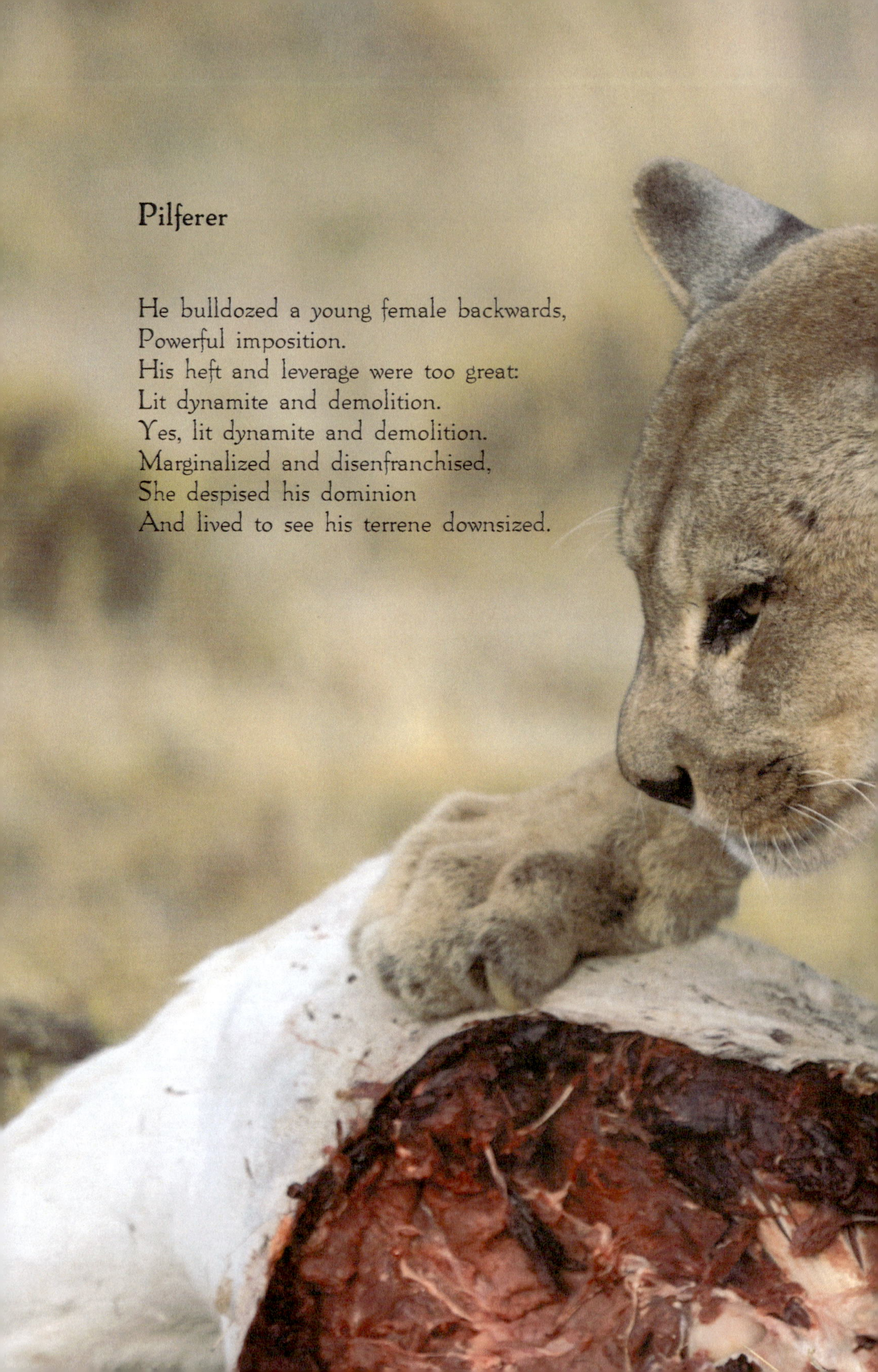

Pilferer

He bulldozed a young female backwards,
Powerful imposition.
His heft and leverage were too great:
Lit dynamite and demolition.
Yes, lit dynamite and demolition.
Marginalized and disenfranchised,
She despised his dominion
And lived to see his terrene downsized.

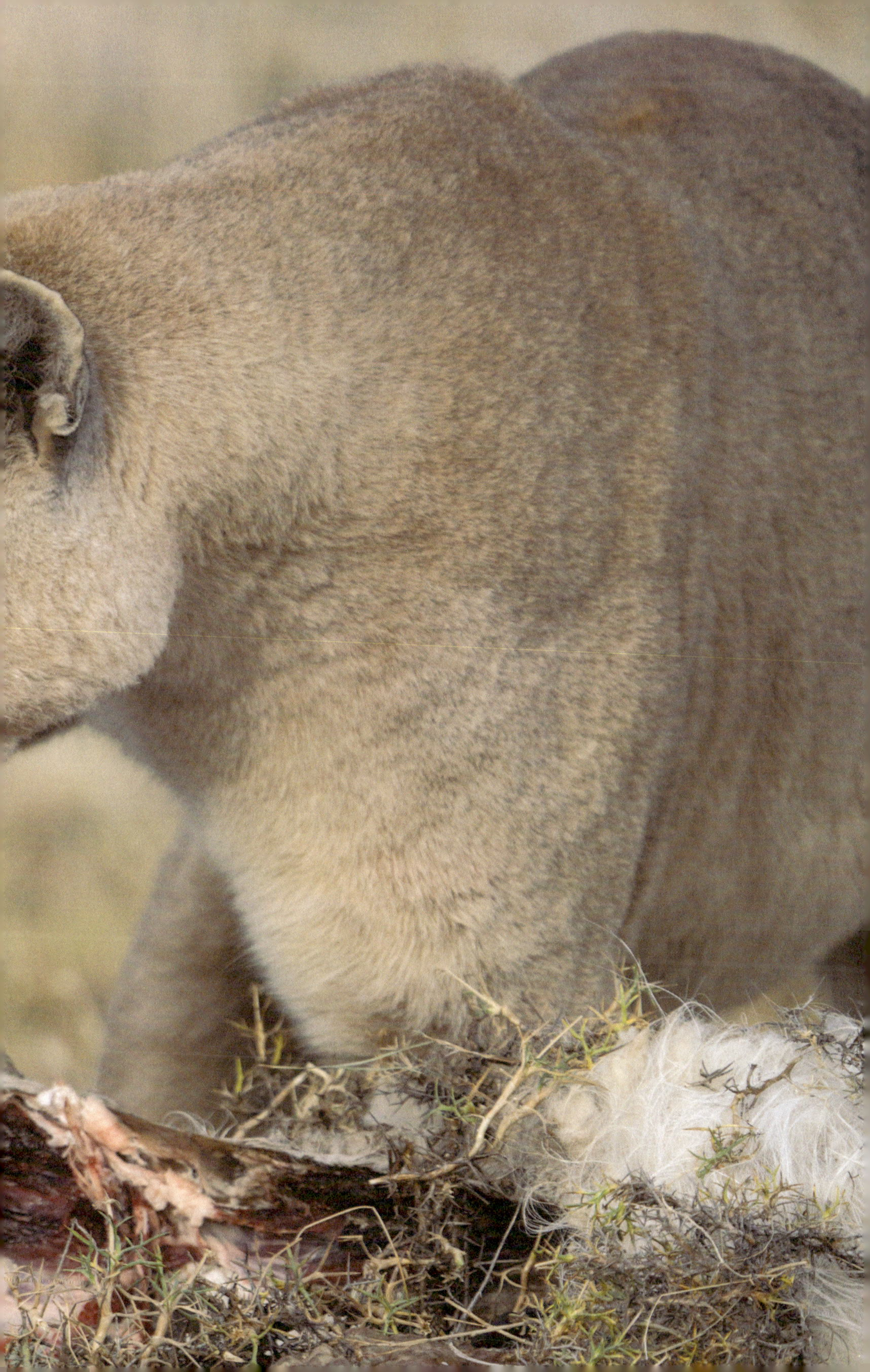

Contusions

Mother bruised by hoof kicks, cut by rocks,
But dragged chulengo hours.
Her cubs greeted her in happy shock.
Woman fixed wounds, empowered.
Yes, woman fixed wounds, empowered.
Cubs hungrily devoured carcass.
She had completed her self-study
And slowly traversed the yellow grass.

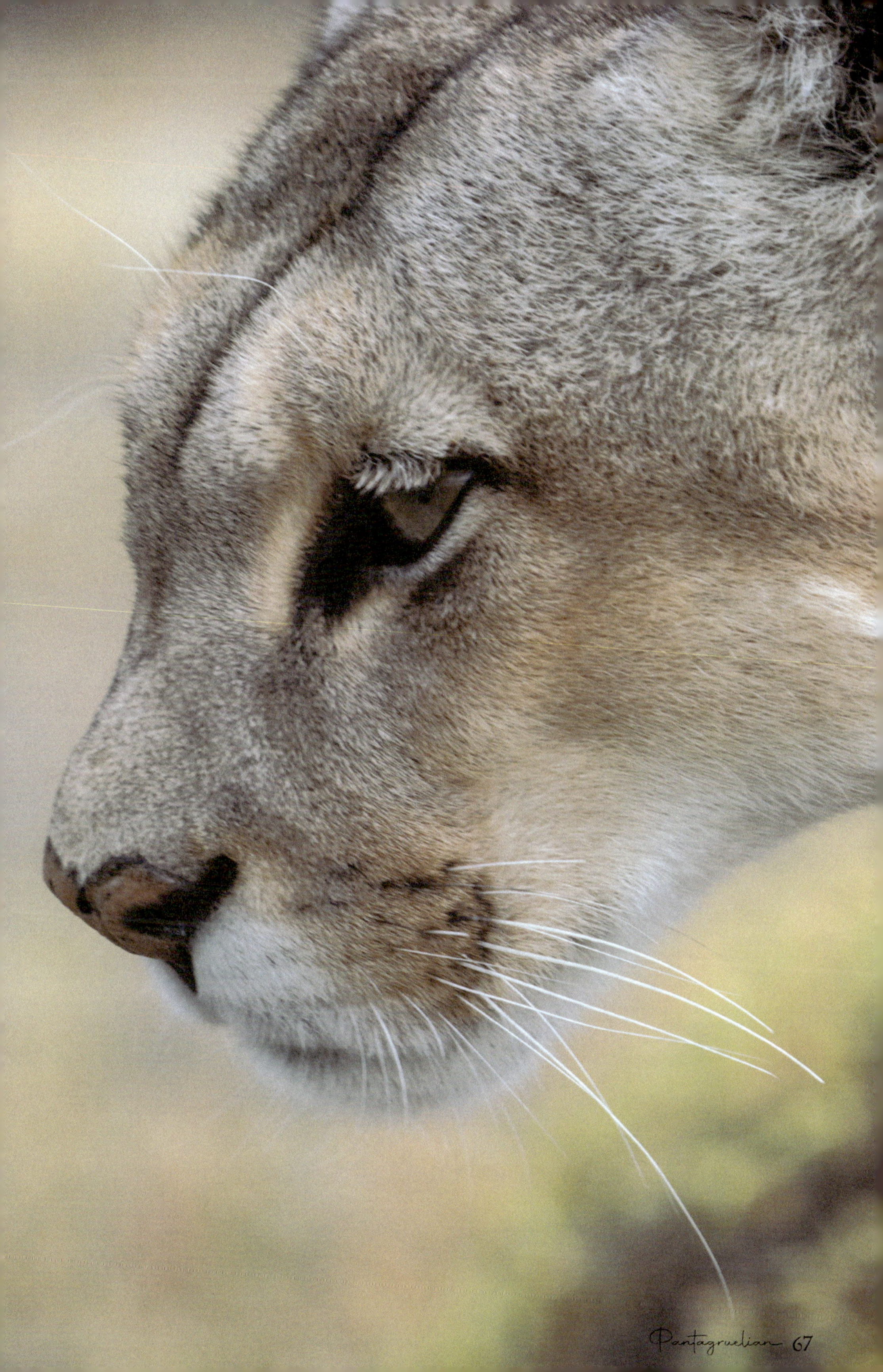
Pantagruelian 67

Driven Out

No warning. Mother berated them
Like they were pariahs; scared.
She chased them fiercely down the hillside.
Her anger expressed her care.
Yes, her anger expressed her care
But they accepted and understood,
Scattering in three trajectories,
Slingshot from childhood to adulthood.

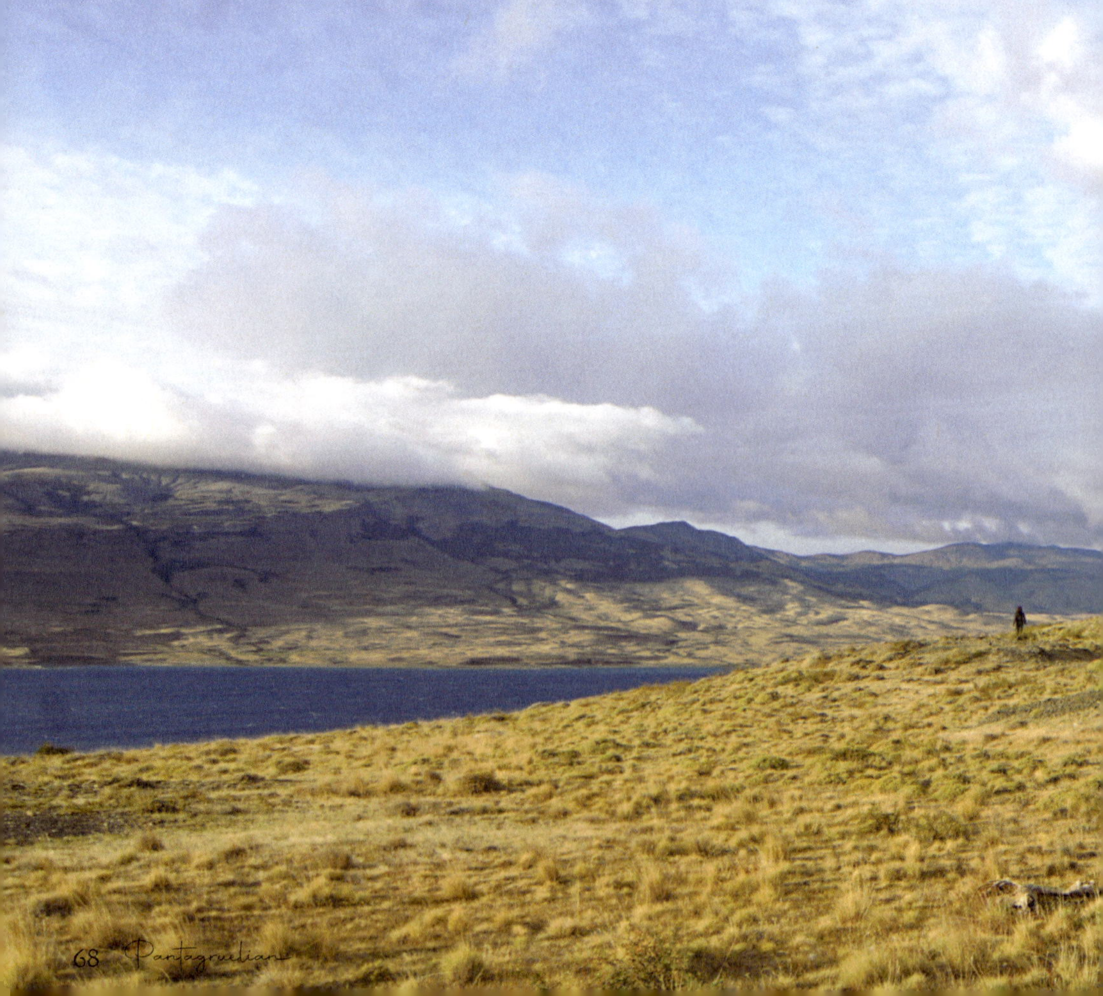

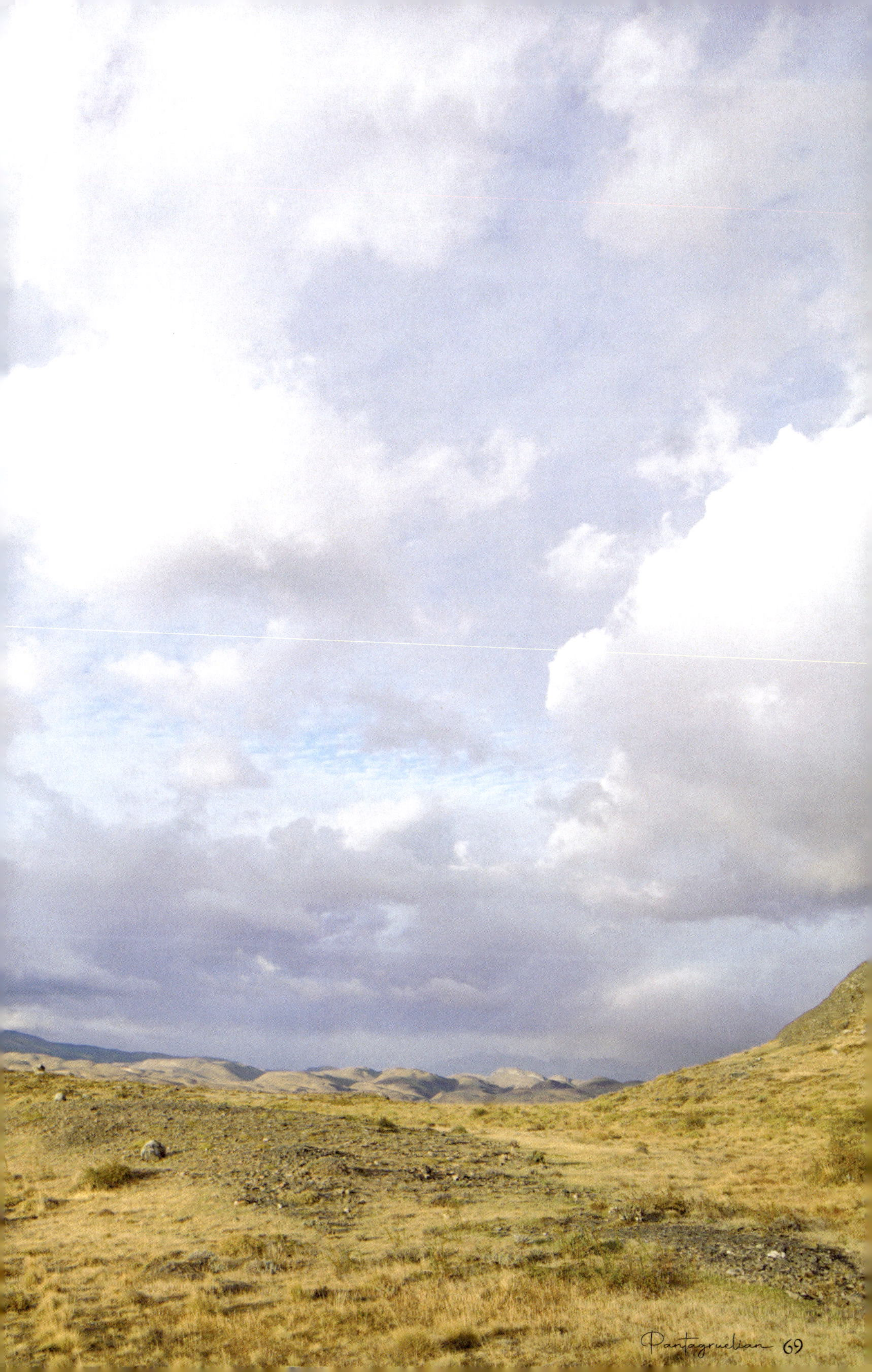
Pantagruelian 69

Glacial Flour

Cyan blue was the tint of fine silt,
Glacial erosion, ground rock
Particles, purest degradation.
Hubris stripped. Humbleness stocked.
Yes, hubris stripped. Humbleness stocked.
Pumas smoothed her callousness,
Scraped away unfriendliness, distrust,
established bluest lake of noblesse.

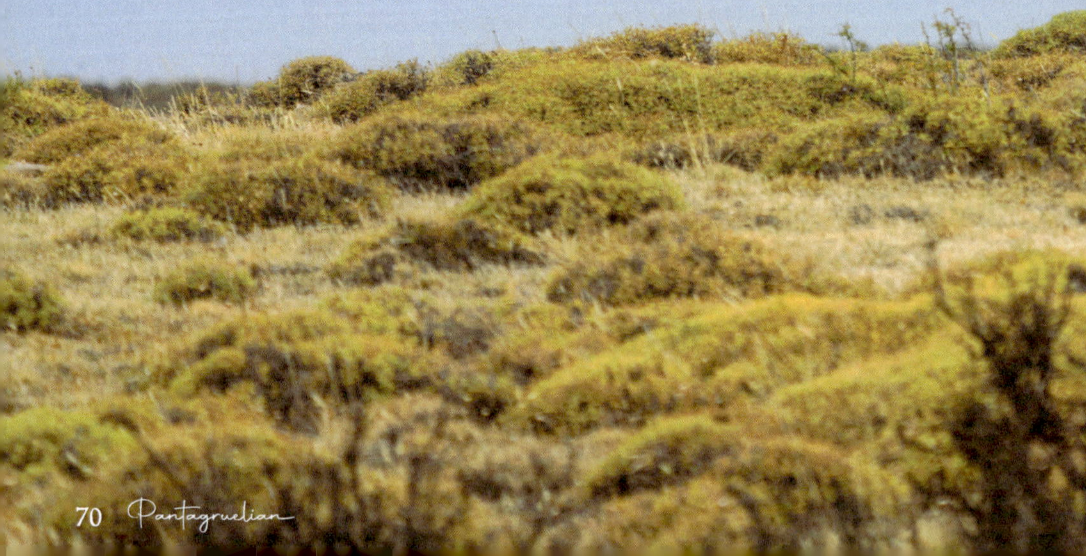

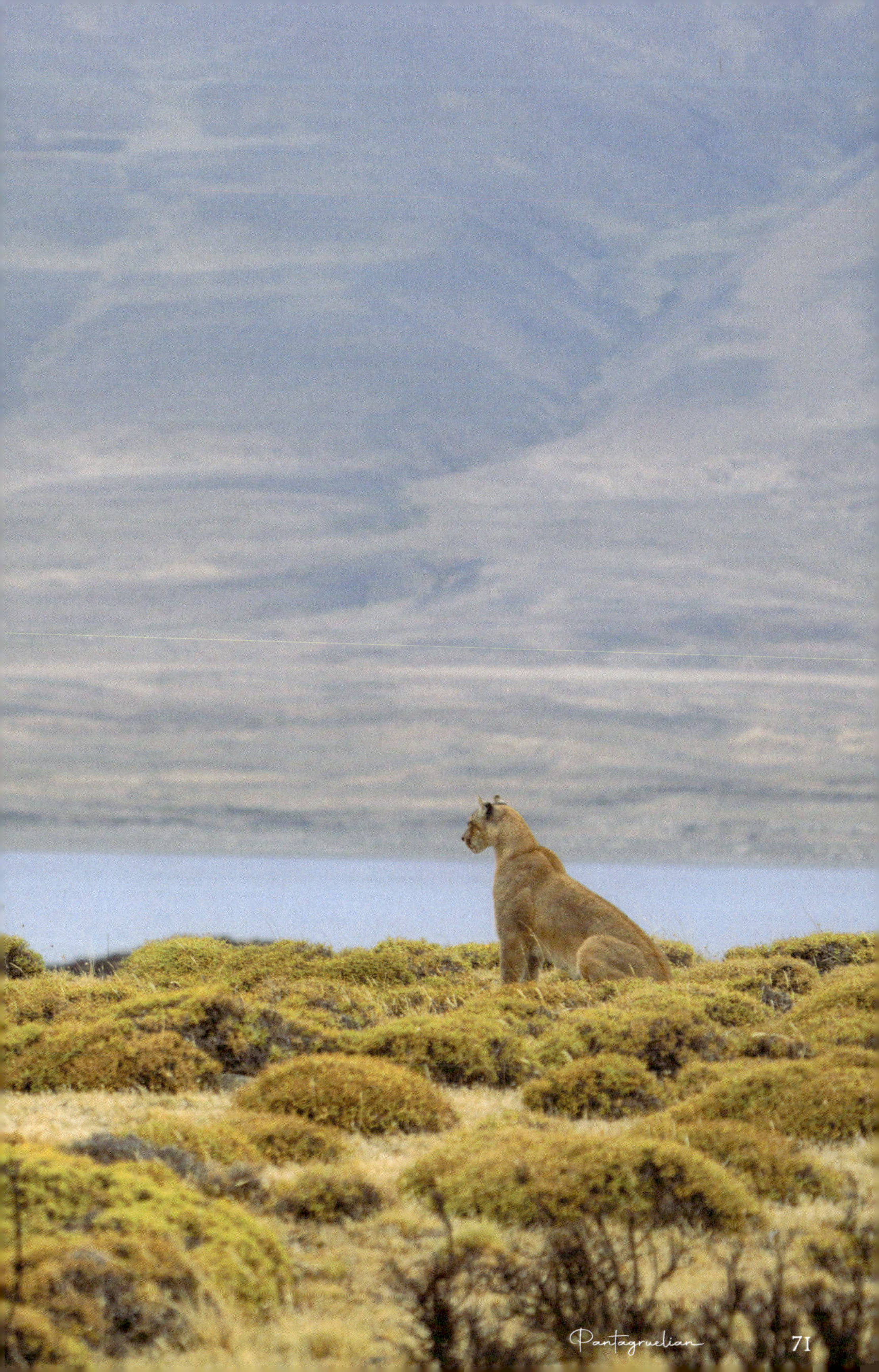
Pantagruelian

Wind-Shaped Trees

Haut monde no longer contorted her
Noted beech trees gnarled, frozen
By force, seemingly curled by wire.
"I'm mata barrarosa.
Yes, I'm mata barrarosa,
Speaking truth-thorns, spreading wider each
Day, a mat of interconnection,
Seeking to renovate and unteach."

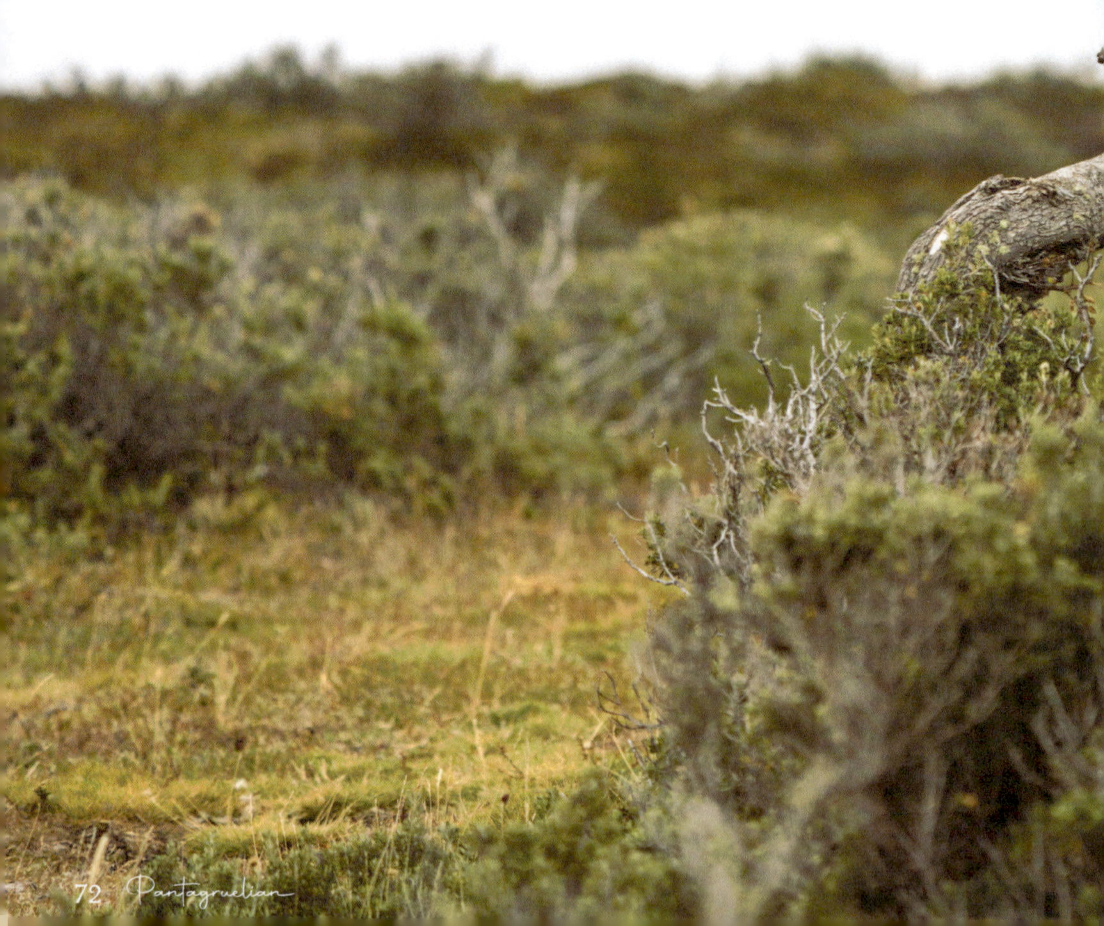

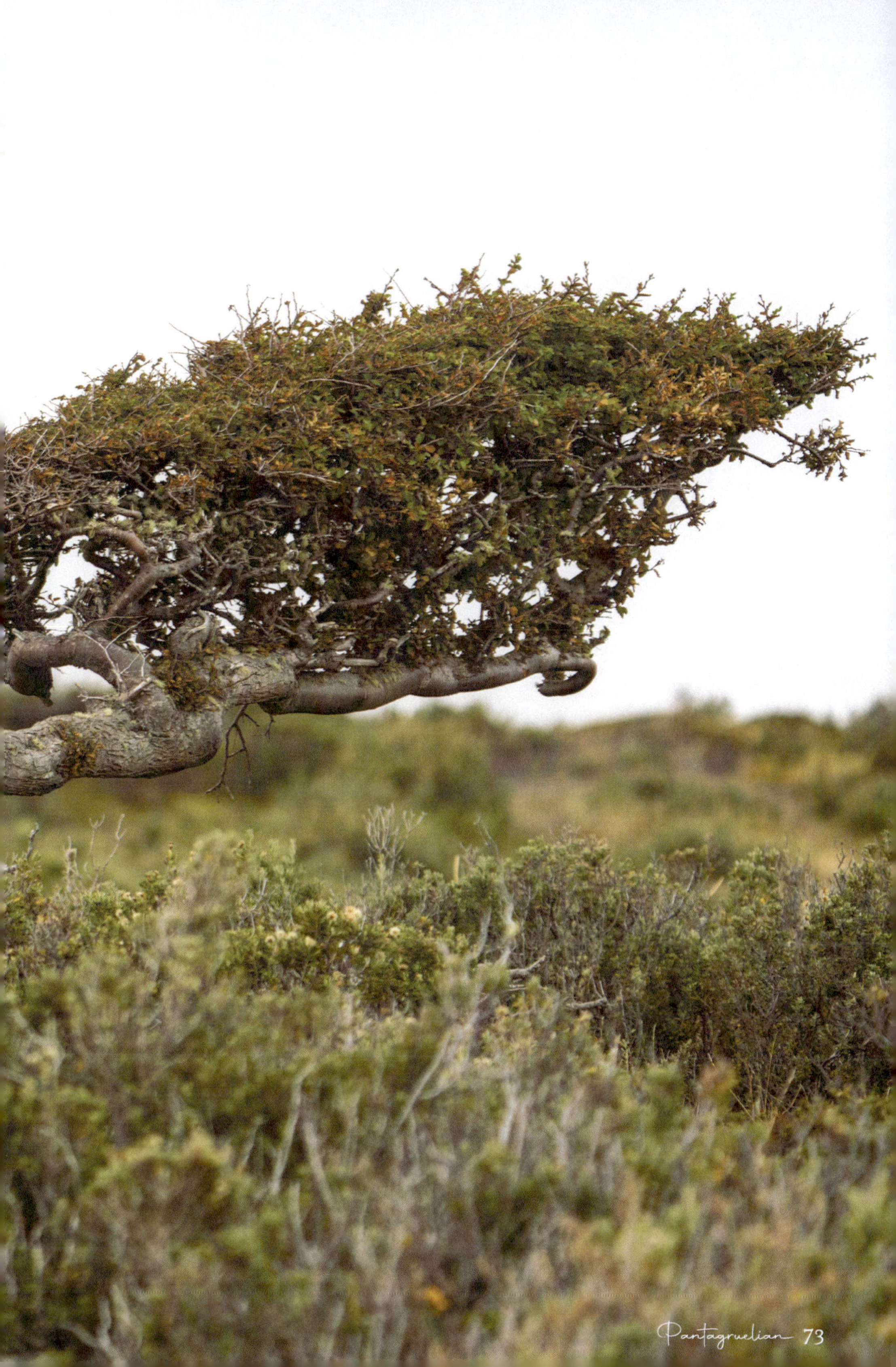
Pantagruelian 73

The One Who Sleeps in Caves with Pumas

Some said she's a speck in the eye,
A guardian, an outlaw,
A figment, a lone lit filament,
A shapeshift caracara.
Yes, a shapeshift caracara
Drifting like a recycled shadow
Adjacent to the gravel ranch road,
Ready to undo the status quo.

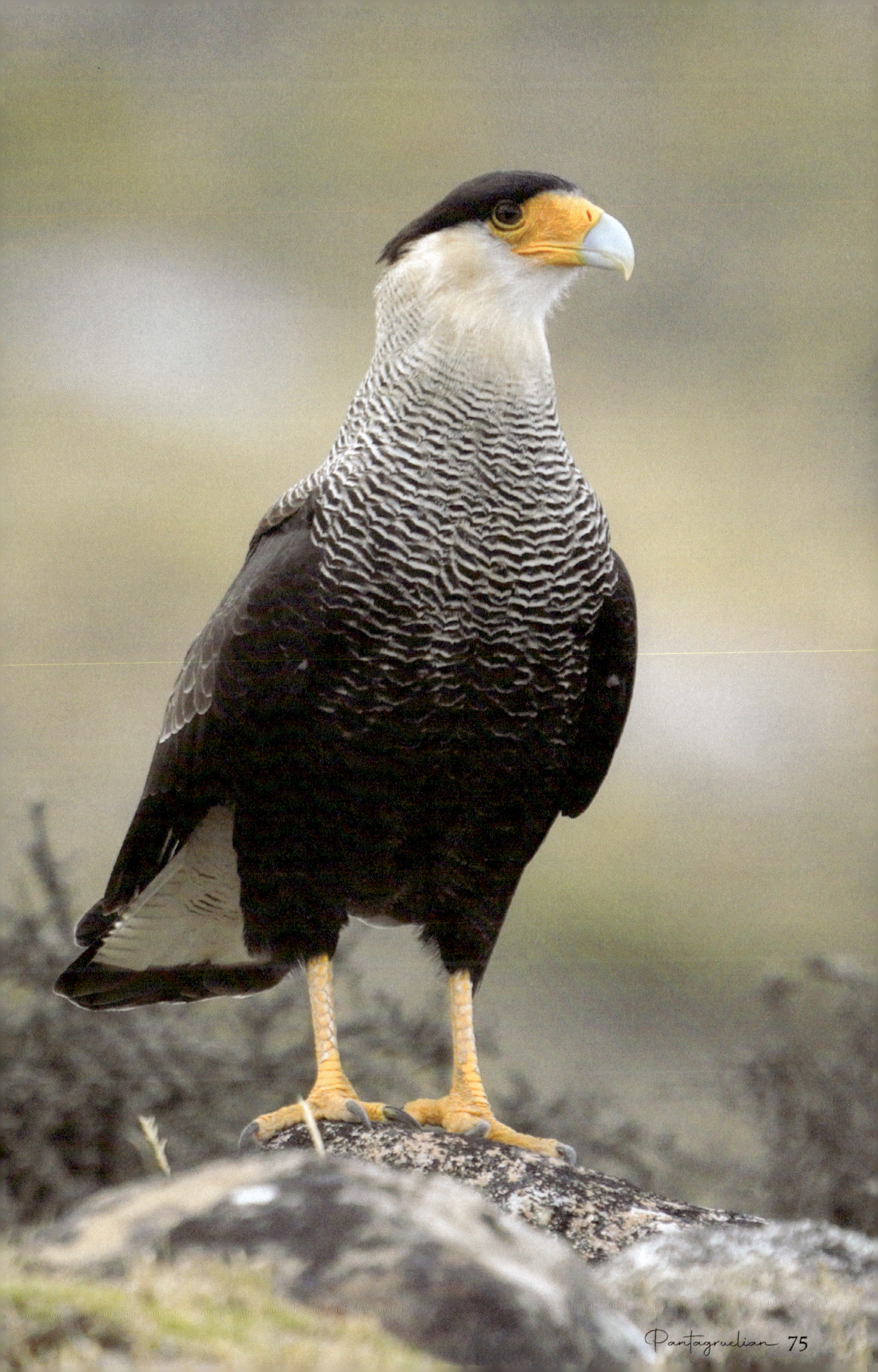
Pantagruelian 75

Purist Tracker

Asked a rancher to be a tracker,
Booked tourist tourist tourist;
Purist bent on making pumas matter.
Fences destroyed; stock shifted.
Yes, fences destroyed; stock shifted:
Sheep gone, cattle rotated, guarded
By dogs. Poaching aborted by heirs.
Paradigm spent. Old ways discarded.

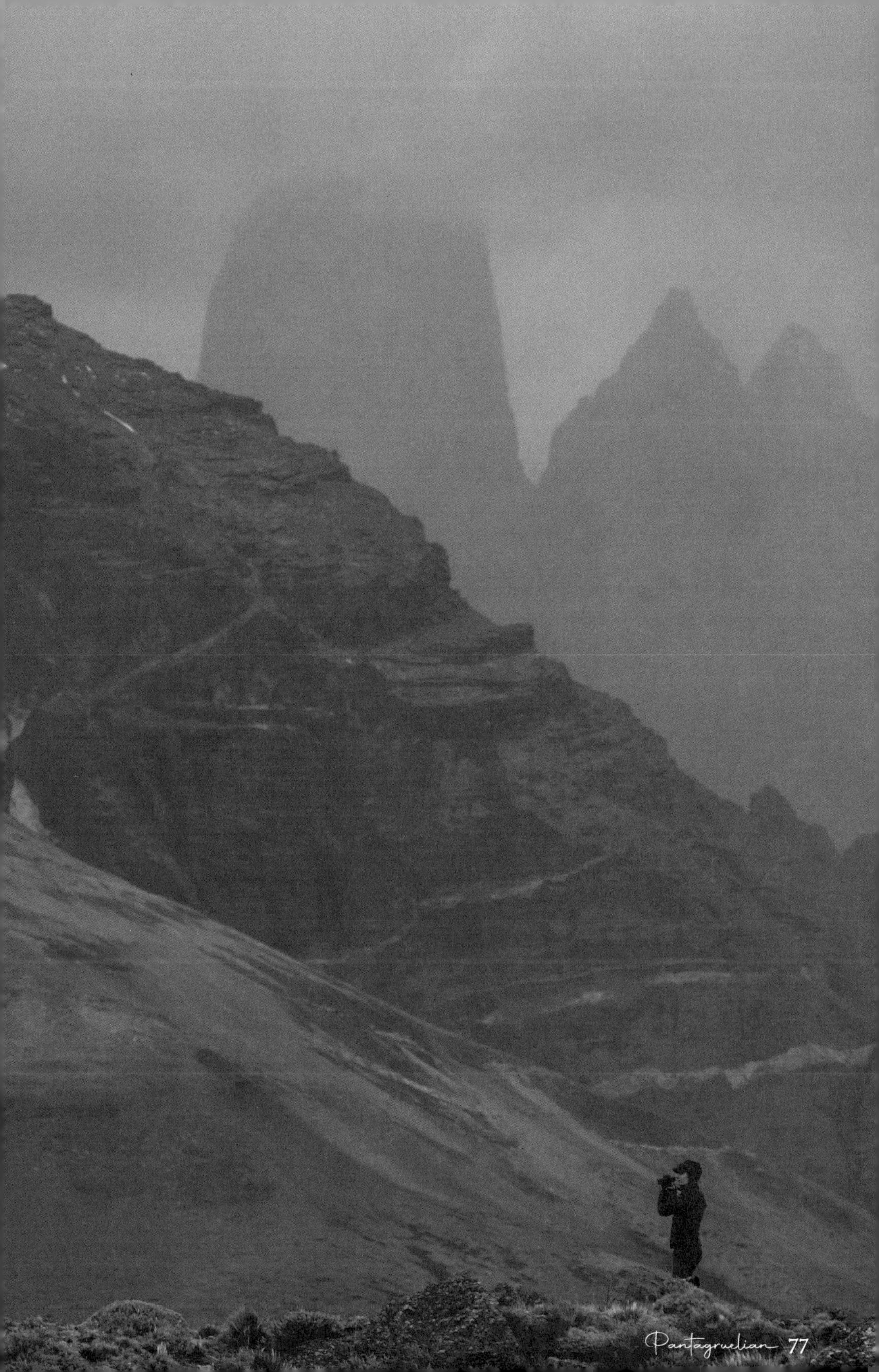
Pantagruelian 77

Hardened Sheep in the Valley

Storms froze whole herds of sheep in their sleep.
Left carcasses strewn like white
Stones. In spring, bones were winnowed, scattered.
Out of crisis comes insight.
Yes, out of crisis comes insight.
Ranchers embraced the charm of pumas,
Denounced old grindstones and artefacts,
Rewrote centuries of bourgeois law.

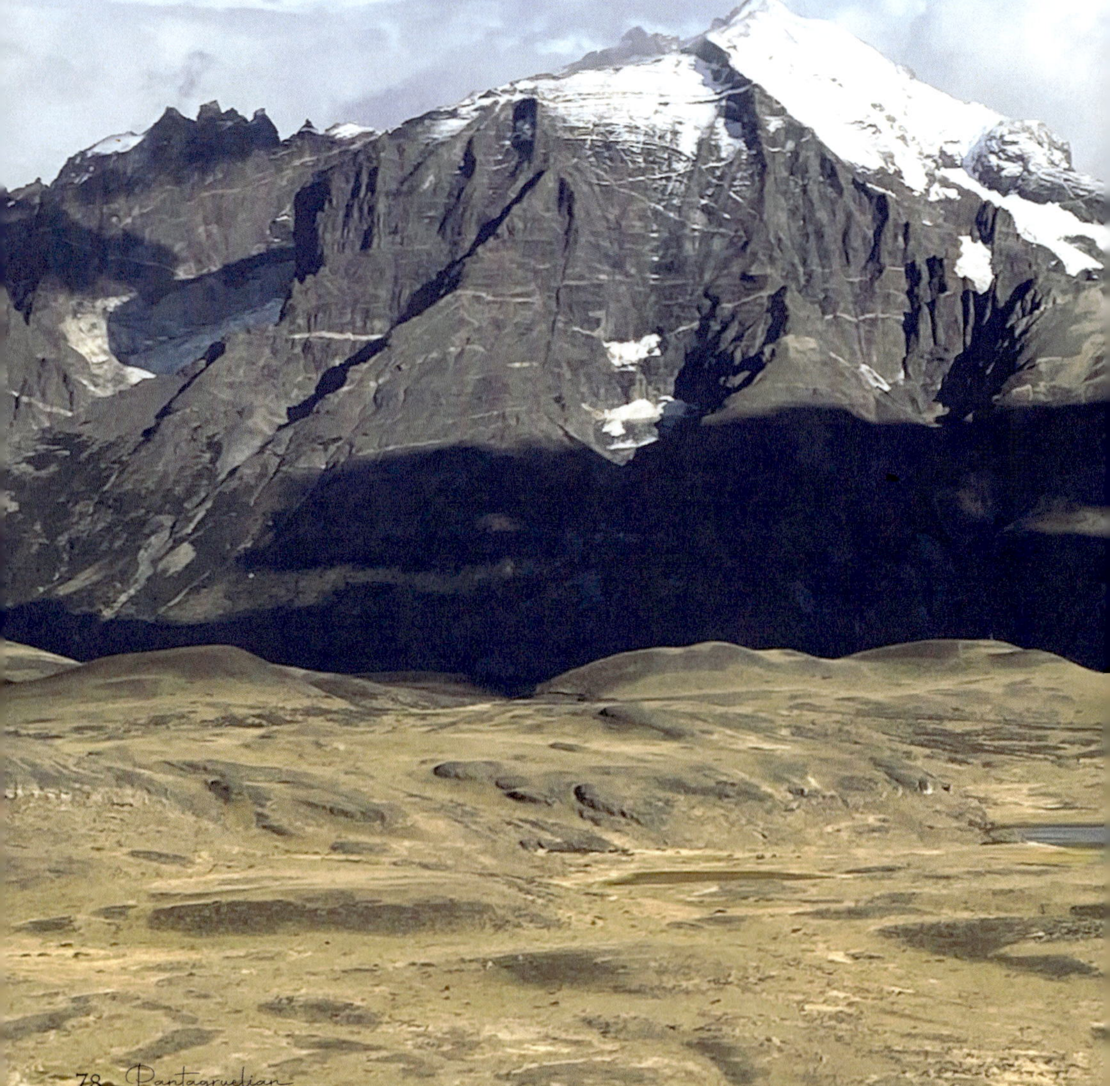

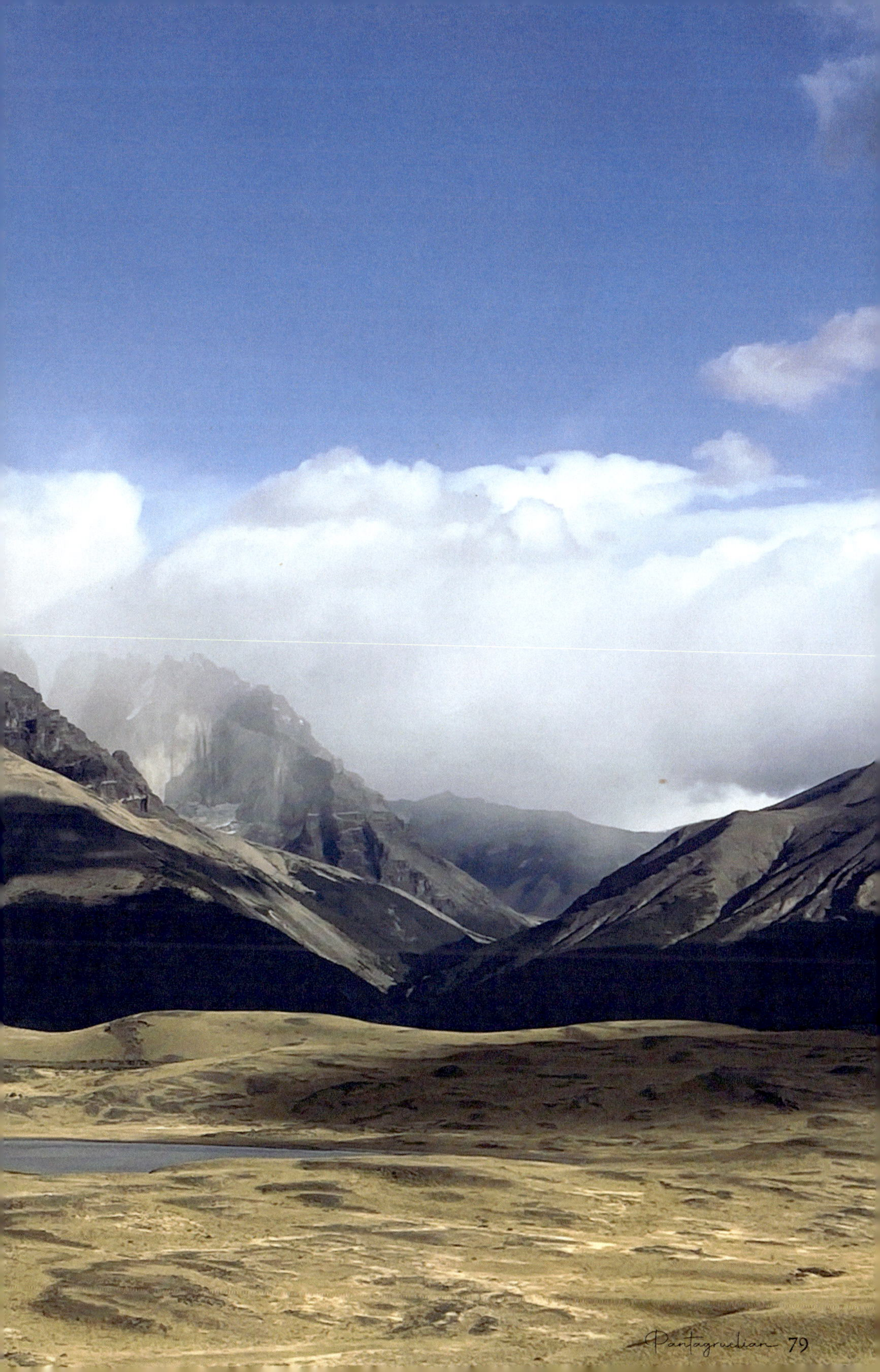
Pantagruelian 79

Crackerjack Tracker

She smelled kills kilometers away
And territory confines
Through urine-marked notro spray.
Knew 80 pumas by sight.
Yes, knew 80 pumas by sight.
Read land like runes, a clairvoyant,
With her feyness and remote viewing,
Predicted domain fights, courtships, hunts.

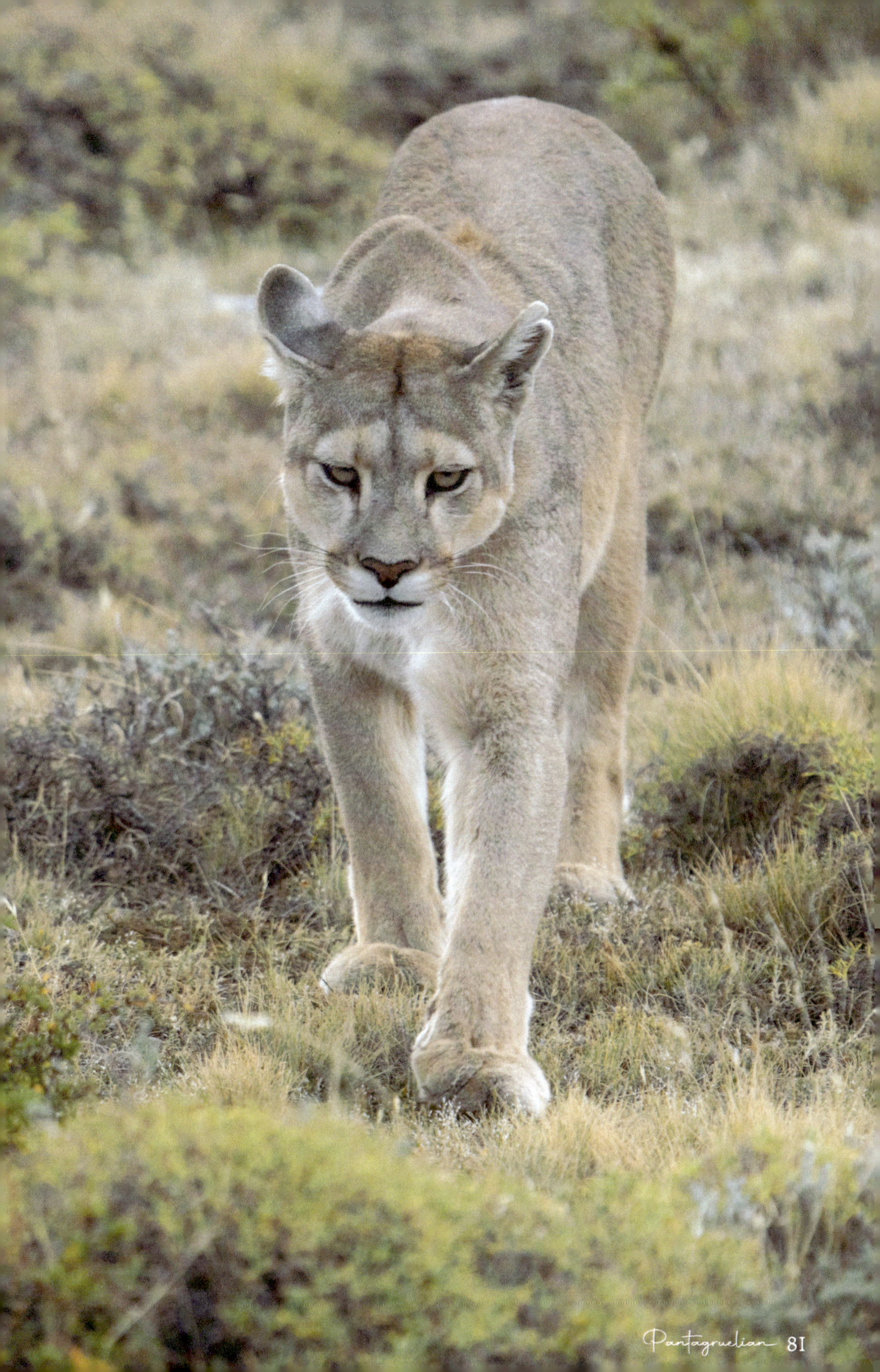
Pantagruelian 81

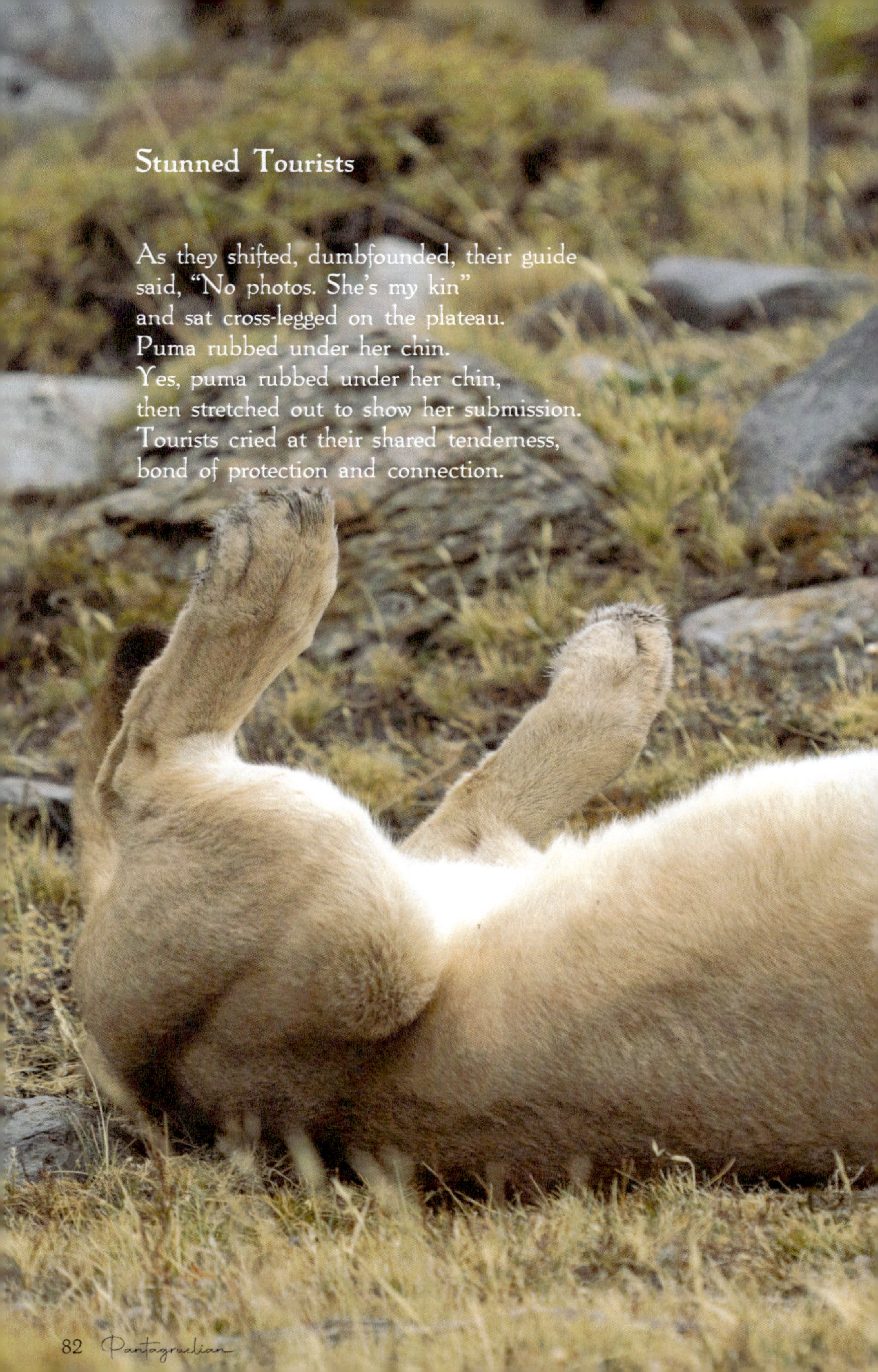

Stunned Tourists

As they shifted, dumbfounded, their guide
said, "No photos. She's my kin"
and sat cross-legged on the plateau.
Puma rubbed under her chin.
Yes, puma rubbed under her chin,
then stretched out to show her submission.
Tourists cried at their shared tenderness,
bond of protection and connection.

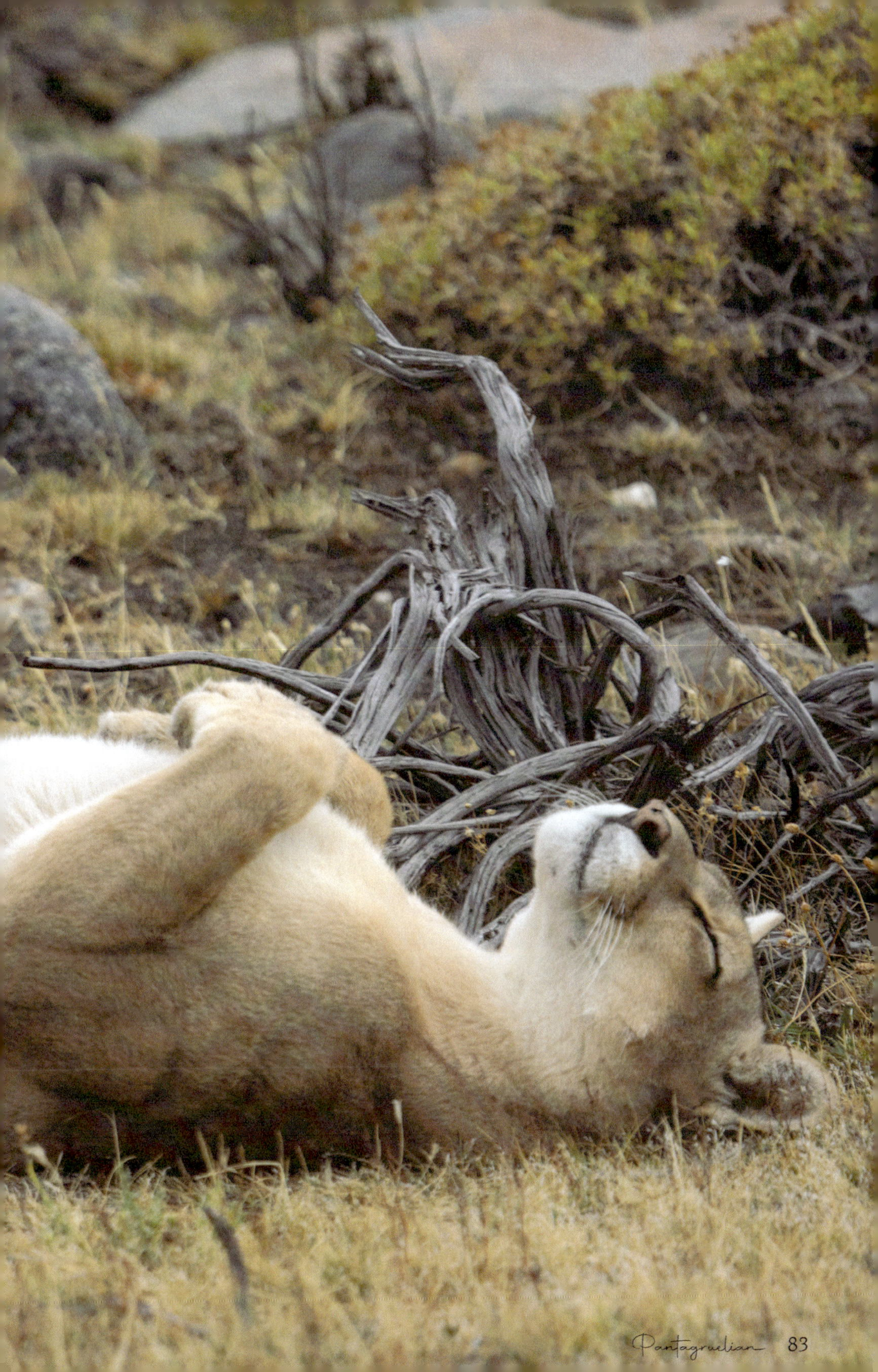

Pantagruelian

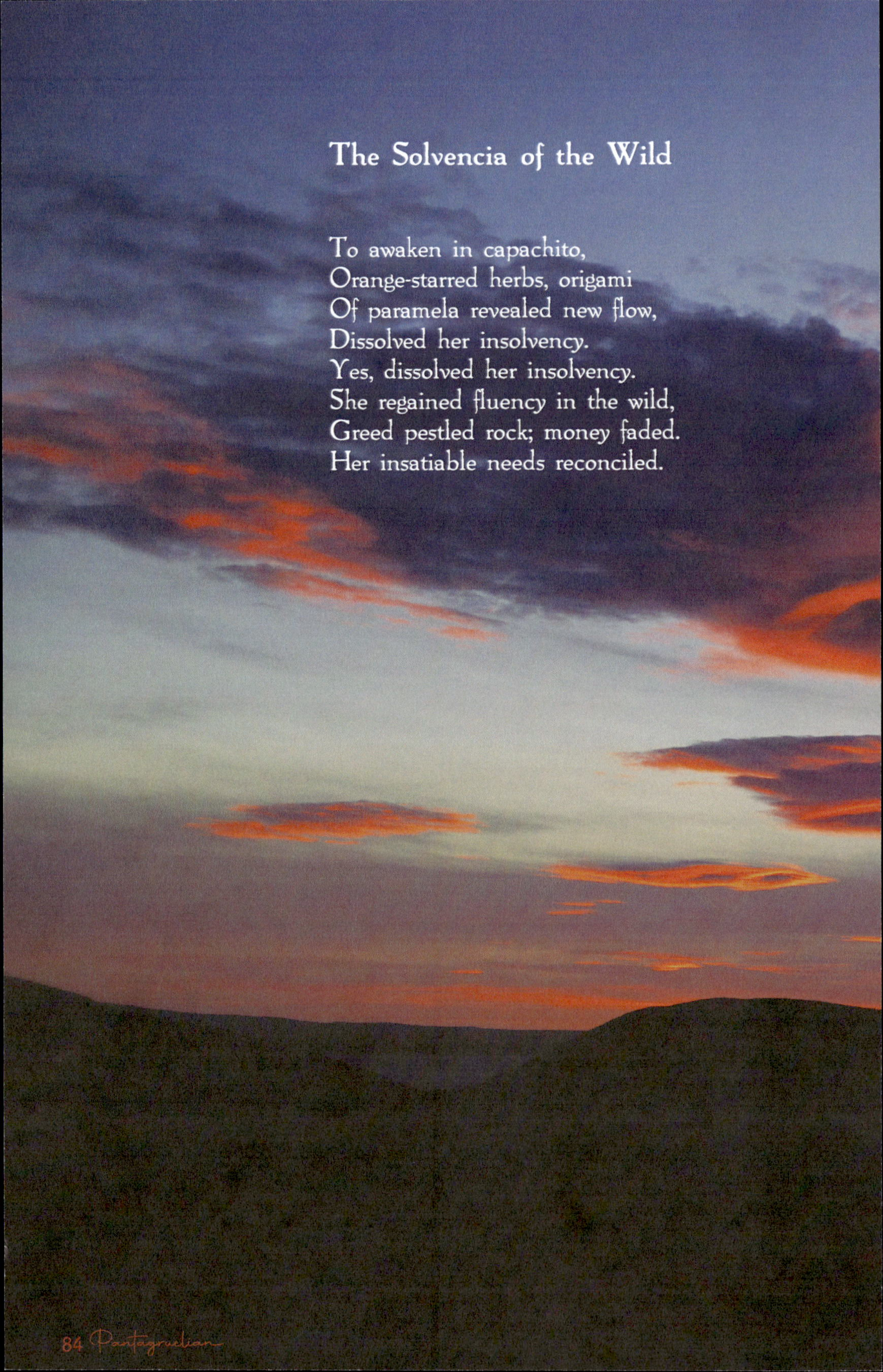

The Solvencia of the Wild

To awaken in capachito,
Orange-starred herbs, origami
Of paramela revealed new flow,
Dissolved her insolvency.
Yes, dissolved her insolvency.
She regained fluency in the wild,
Greed pestled rock; money faded.
Her insatiable needs reconciled.

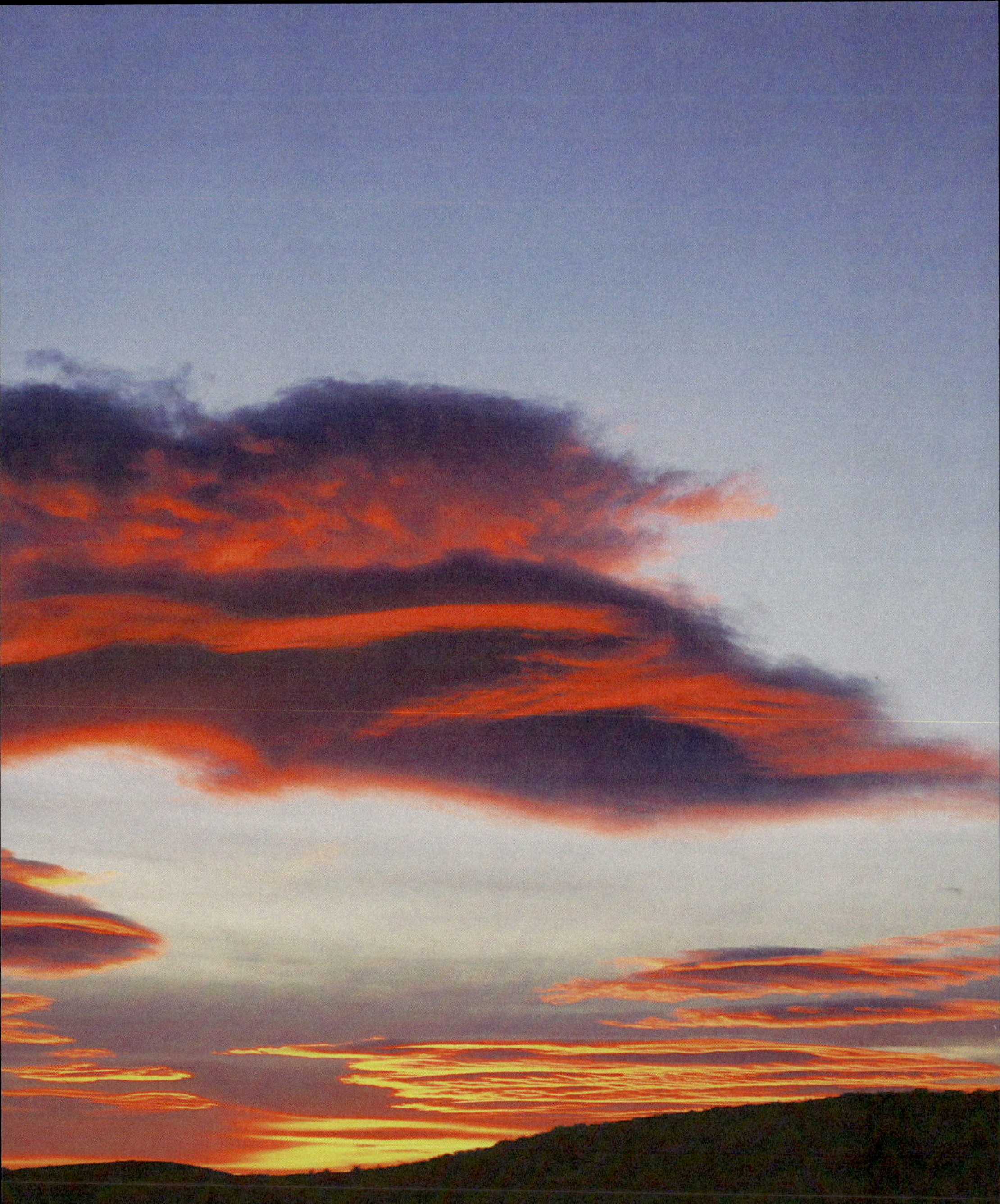

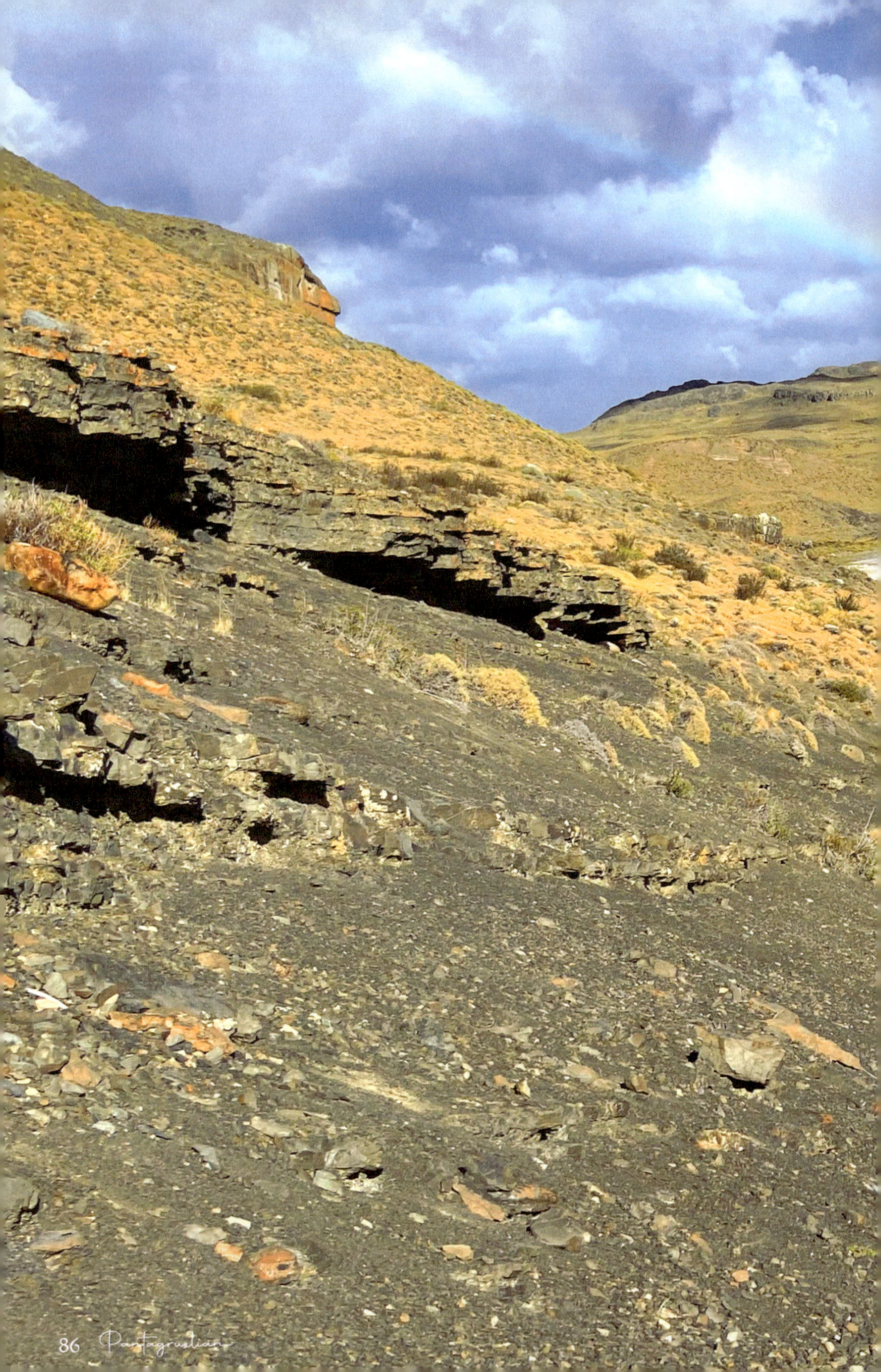

 Pantagruelism

About the Author:

Paul Brooke provides a unique window into understanding pumas by photographing and documenting their behavior in this spectacular region. He is the author of seven other books including *Jaguars of the Northern Pantanal: Panthera onca at the Meeting of the Waters*, *Sirens and Seriemas: Photographs and Poems of the Amazon and Pantanal*, *Light and Matter: Photographs and Poems of Iowa*, *Meditations on Egrets: Photographs and Poems of Sanibel Island*, *Arm Wrestling at the Iowa State Fair*, *The Skáld the Drukkin Tröllaukin: Photographs and Poems of Iceland*, and *The Cities of the Plains: An Anthology of Iowa Artists and Poets*.

His poetry has appeared in journals such as *Scientific American*, *The North American Review* and *The Antioch Review*, while his photography has been exhibited across the United States and featured in *Audubon* and *Wild Planet* magazines. He serves on the Board for the North American Nature Photography Association. This project was funded with grants from the Iowa Arts Council and The Puffin Foundation.

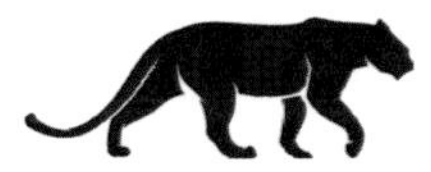

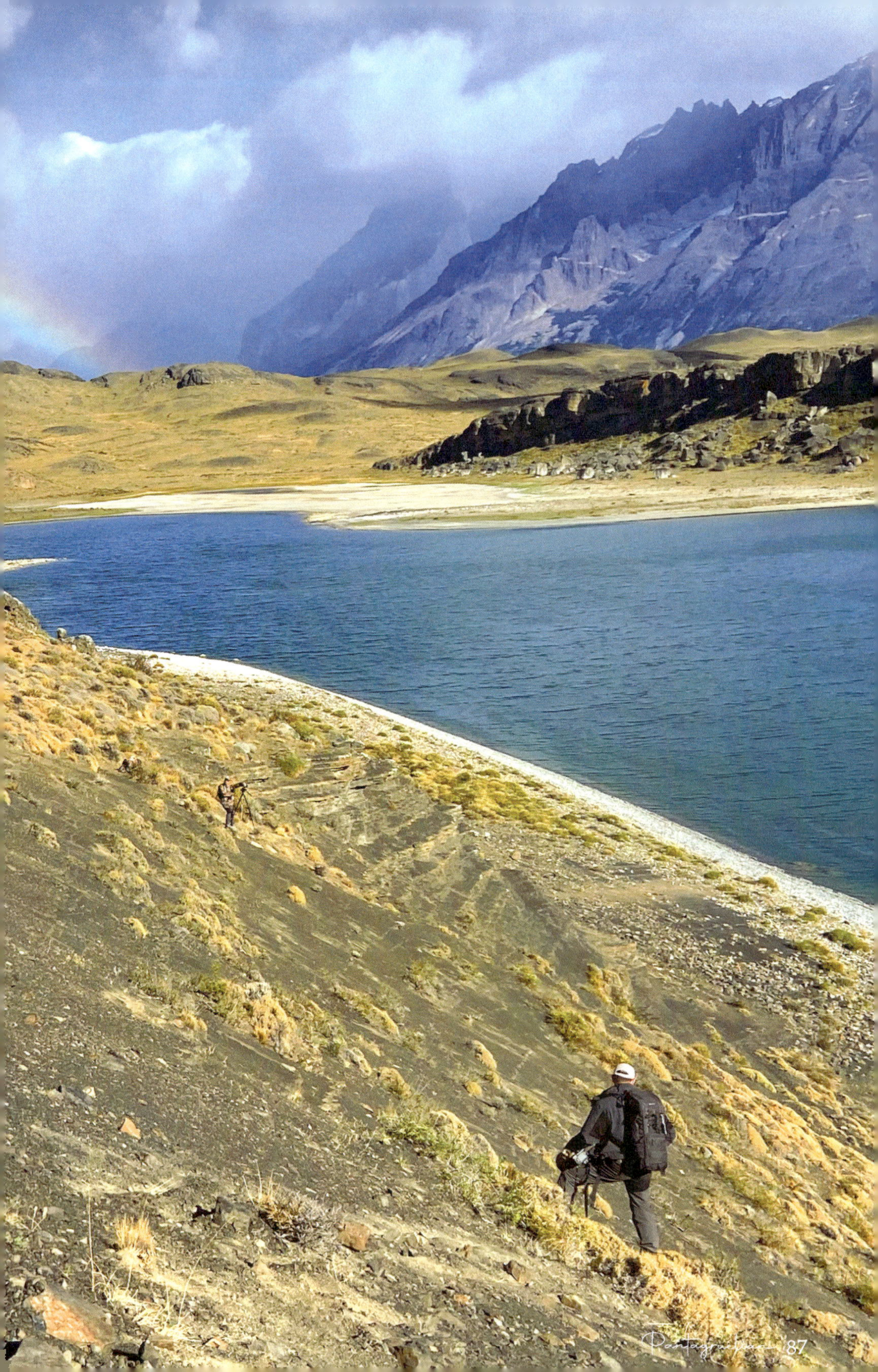

Patagonia 2006 '87

* 9 7 8 1 7 3 7 7 8 0 8 7 8 *